FREEDOM
FROM FEAR AND PANIC

3/6/17

Grace Nichols

My dear sister Sue!
My prayer is that this book will
guide you into a more indepht
study of Gods Word teaching you
to do spiritual warfare against
our greatest enemy! May our Lord
unfold his truths to you that
will guide you into that more
than abundant life that Jesus
came to give! Love your sister-Grace

ISBN 978-1-68197-900-7 (Paperback)
ISBN 978-1-68197-902-1 (Hard Cover)
ISBN 978-1-68197-901-4 (Digital)

Christian Faith Publishing, Inc.
296 Chestnut Street
Meadville, PA 16335
www.christianfaithpublishing.com

Printed in the United States of America

DEDICATION

I would like to dedicate this book, *Freedom from Fear and Panic* to my eldest brother, Joseph. I know you have had your struggles in this area, and I thank God for your endurance and steadfastness—that despite opposition, you continue to stand upon God's Word!

My prayer is that God will open your eyes of understanding even more in this area of suffering so that you can be all you can be for him, while enjoying the freedom and liberty Jesus Christ gave his life for.

In Jesus's name, amen.

Love, your sister, Grace

I want to dedicate this book also to my two beloved daughters Michella and Kayanna.

I am so very proud and admire your Christian faith and stand.

There is nothing more important or valuable than knowing and walking in the truth of God's Word.

My hope is that upon reading this book that our God will open up your eyes even more in understanding more of life's battles. And that you to will learn how to overcome any and all attacks from our enemy by following the Lord's instructions that he sets forth in his Word. That you can utilize the tools of wisdom that will help you to achieve the walk of liberty that sets us free that Jesus came to give.

I love you, Mom

INTRODUCTION

If you are a person reading this book because you can relate and are suffering from fear and panic in your life but have not accepted Jesus as your Lord and Savior, then it is vitally important that you do so for your freedom, deliverance, and salvation.

In Romans 10:9–11, it states, "Because if you acknowledge and confess with your lips that Jesus is Lord and in your heart believe [adhere, to trust in and rely on the truth] that God raised him from the dead, you will be saved." (v. 9)

"For with the heart, a person believes [adheres to, trusts in, and relies on Christ] and so is justified [declared righteous, acceptable to God], and with the mouth he confesses [declares openly and speaks out freely his faith] and confirms [his] salvation." (v. 10)

"The Scripture says, No man who believes in him [who adheres to, relies on and trusts in him] will [ever] be put to shame or be disappointed." (v. 11)

So, let's begin here as God instructs. Say aloud these words: Dear, Lord Jesus, I know I am a sinner, and I ask for your forgiveness. I believe you died for my sins and rose from the dead. I trust and follow you as my Lord and Savior. Guide my life and help me to do your will. In Jesus name, Amen.

Jesus is your Savior! A Savior is defined as one who saves from destruction, and Jesus is the one who sets us free!

It is not God's will for us, his children, to be living our lives in fear and panic but on the contrary, to have his peace, joy, and power in any and all circumstances. After all, isn't that one of the reasons Jesus endured the cross "to set the captives free"?

Then, why do so many people battle and struggle in these areas? Because they do not know the truth—the truth that will set them free! The Bible clearly states in

John 8:32, "And you shall know the truth and the truth shall set you free!" The answer of how to obtain this freedom is indeed found in the Word of God! There are many revelations in the Word of God, things that God wants you to know. There are keys to living the abundant life that he desires for you to have.

As you begin to read and study, getting deeper into God's Word, you'll discover how to achieve your freedom from the fear and panic that has kept you bound. God will unfold to you the many truths and insights that will be key to your success, therefore bringing about freedom. It is God's absolute will that you be free from anything that controls, hinders, binds, or keeps you from being all you can be.

Next, I would like to encourage that you get some materials for this study on the road to your freedom: an Amplified Bible, *Webster Dictionary* (preferably Collegiate), pens and markers, and index cards. This version of the Bible and dictionary is what I used mainly in my study. You will want to write down many things and scriptures on the index cards as the Lord leads you, so you can pull them out and read them throughout your day to keep them in the forefront of your mind. This will be vitally important to your success.

Chapter
1

You Are not Going Crazy

Fear is an unpleasant, often strong, emotion caused by anticipation or awareness of danger—an anxious concern, producing dread, fright, alarm, panic, and tremors. Panic is a sudden, overpowering fright, a sudden unreasonable terror. When these two things attack our bodies and minds, they seem to take control and keep you frozen in your steps, almost paralyzing your every move.

Over the years, I have seen people unable to cope with these attacks. The attacks would become so severe that they would keep them bound in their homes and unable to sleep for days at a time. Many people, desperate in their need for comfort, resort to alcohol and drugs to put a Band-Aid—if you will—on their situation. This may bring temporary relief but still not receiving total and complete freedom, ease or rest. Oftentimes, these Band-Aids bring more problems to their health and enslave them further to their situation.

You are not going crazy! You are God's masterpiece, and he did not create—nor was it his desire—for you to live this way! On the contrary, it is his complete will for you to have joy, peace, and confidence in every situation. He wants you to be set free from anything that controls or binds us.

Freedom is liberation from slavery or restraint or from the power of another.

WHERE DO THESE ATTACKS ORIGINATE?

Before we begin to talk about this freedom, first let me emphasize that God is well aware of these attacks and the opposing forces behind them. Over and over, in the Word, he addresses this very subject and gives full instructions on how to obtain freedom.

2 Timothy 1:7 states, "For God did not give us a spirit of timidity [of cowardice, of craven and cringing and fawning fear] but he has given us a spirit of power and of love and of a calm and well-balanced mind and discipline and self-control."

So let's see, if God did not subject us to this, then where does it come from? David knew exactly where as he wrote the following in the book of Psalm.

Psalm 55:3–6 states, "And I am distracted at the noise of the enemy because of the oppression [web: a sense of being weighed down in body or mind by an unjust or cruel exercise of authority or power] and threats of the wicked; for they would cast trouble upon me and in wrath [web: strong, vengeful anger] they persecute [web: to cause to suffer because of one's beliefs with annoying, persistent attacks] me." (v. 3)

"My heart is grievously pained within me and the terrors of death have fallen upon me. (v. 4)

"Fear and trembling have come upon me; horror [web: calculated to inspire feelings of dread and to cause one to tremble] and fright [web: something strange bringing about fear] have overwhelmed me. (v. 5)

"And I say, oh that I had wings like a dove! I would fly away and be at rest." (v. 6)

Wow! Can you believe it? Even David had experienced these same emotions. How many of us just want to run and fly away when fear and panic strike? David knew full well where the attacks came from when he stated in verse 3 that he was distracted by the noise of the enemy! This is a huge revelation God gives us here. He wants us to be fully aware of who is attacking us and why. As a believer, we know full well who our enemy is, Satan. Why is Satan persecuting us? Look at verse 3 again, "causes us to suffer because of our beliefs." Beliefs in what? In God, our Lord Jesus Christ, his Word and because he hates all God has created.

I too, like you, was attacked by this same oppression out of the blue one day. I had been hit with panic attacks previously in my life, but it had only seemed to be for a fleeting moment here and there before it quickly went away. But this time, it was different. I awoke to find myself in a state of panic with my heart racing and my body trembling. It was to the point that I couldn't even lie there, and I began pacing the floor for hours. I couldn't even focus on the Word to read. Naturally, I cried out to God, "Help me, Lord!" I asked, "What is going on? What in the world is this? Am I going crazy?" I tried to lay down several times and calm myself, but each time, I found myself up and pacing the floor again in complete and total panic. Needless to say, I couldn't sleep all night. I then started to get angry with God. Why are you allowing this on me? Since that evening, the attacks came, oppressing me even during the day and repeated night after night. I was a believer and had been for many years, and I knew that Satan had no rights over me. I relentlessly prayed day after day and asked the Lord to let me be able to read and just focus on his Word. He answered my prayer, and I began doing just that. I had talked with other people about what I was going through, and to my amazement, many of them began telling me that they were experiencing this same thing. Even though I had heard of people going through this over the years, I was shocked to hear how many people are suffering presently from anxiety and panic.

A lot of women suggested that I was going through menopause due to the related symptoms. This led me on a search and study of menopause, and I found that these were indeed the same signs and symptoms that I was experiencing. However, something still troubled me. The many people I talked with weren't all women. Some of them, being men, were seemingly plagued by the same torment. In addition, many women I talked with weren't of age yet to be in a menopausal state. There's something wrong here! Why do so many people suffer in this area? Even if you are one of these women suffering or going through menopause, it is not God's will for us to suffer or be in pain. Isn't that what Jesus died for? To bring us back into relationship with God and bring us comfort and peace while we are here?

God has revealed to me that I was in a huge spiritual battle—one that could not be fought in my own human strength. To me, this was a great revelation! Thus, I began an almost two-year journey into an in-depth study of the Word of God. My mission was not only to aid myself in overcoming this spiritual battle, but also a heartfelt intent to help others, like you, who are going through this, believing God on his keys to obtaining the freedom that he promises through Jesus Christ, our Lord. Well, God is faithful as he has promised and has shown me many things that prompted me to write this book.

Before reading on, I encourage you to get some index cards as this was a vital key in receiving freedom from God. As you read, write down verses of scripture and anything the Lord gives you. Read these cards throughout your day while going through these trials, especially before bed and first thing in the morning. I grouped my cards together with a paper clip and when the stack got too large, I started a new bundle. The important thing is that you keep God's Word up in your mind instead of what the devil is attacking your mind with, which I will get into more later during this study.

Chapter
2

God Instructs Us to Pray

It has been said that if people knew how much power there was in prayer, people would be praying twenty-four hours a day, seven days a week.

Well, this is very true! Prayerful lives *are* powerful lives. Prayer actually opens up the floodgates of heaven to empower us to live the lives that God has called us out to live—one of power, peace, love, and joy. So we have to ask ourselves, "Why aren't we?" Why do we live on the contrary: in fear, doubt, anxiety, confusion, and panic? God addresses fret and anxiety in the book of Philippians.

Philippians 4:6–7 states, "Do not fret or have anxiety about anything, but in every circumstance and in everything, by prayer and petition [definite requests], with thanksgiving, continue to make your wants known to God."

Why does God address fretting and anxiety? Because he already knows you are going to be tempted with it. News flash! This is nothing new to God. The devil has been attacking people with this since the beginning of time. I believe fear to be one of the devil's biggest guns, so to speak. The word *fret* here means to suffer emotional strain. Anxiety is an abnormal and overwhelming sense of apprehension and fear often marked by physiological signs such as sweating, tension, and increased pulse.

God also tells us here what to do when being attacked by these emotions when he says in every circumstance and in everything by prayer. The first thing he mentions after fret and anxiety is to pray and petition, which means to ask for something or request. Then, he says "with thanksgiving," meaning a prayer expressing gratitude. So just from this verse alone, we find when being attacked with fret and anxiety, he instructs us to pray and petition by making a specific request and give thanks like we already have it.

CONTINUE TO PRAY

Then, as we read in the latter part of the same verse, it says to continue to make your wants known to God. Obviously, this is not a one-time deal. The word *continue* means to maintain without interruption, carry on, or keep up. Many people, after praying a few times, give up when they don't see results right away. Now we see in the next verse, the promise.

"And God's peace [shall be yours, that tranquil state of a soul assured of its salvation through Christ, and so fearing nothing from God and being content with its earthly lot of whatever sort, that is, that peace] shall be yours which transcends all understanding shall garrison and mount guard over your hearts and minds in Christ Jesus." (v. 7)

The word *transcends* means to rise above or go beyond the limits of the universe or material existence. *Garrison* means to protect or defend as a military post. So, let's re-read that same verse in its deeper meaning. God's peace, which rises above or goes beyond the limits of the universe or material existence of all understanding, shall protect and defend as a military post and mount guard over your hearts and minds in Christ Jesus. All over the Word, God instructs us to PRAY.

Ephesians 6:18a states, "Pray at all times [on every occasion, in every season] in the spirit, with all manner of prayer and entreaty." *Entreaty* means to ask for urgently.

James 5:13a states, "Is anyone among you afflicted [ill-treated, suffering evil]? He should pray." A more in-depth meaning of the word *afflicted* here means to distress so severely as to cause persistent suffering or anguish. Let's read on.

1 Thessalonians 5:17 states, "Be unceasing in prayer [praying perseveringly]." The word *unceasing* means continuous.

EVEN JESUS PRAYED CONTINUOUSLY

Even Jesus knew the great power of prayer and spent much of his time doing just that, without ceasing. He gives us an account of this in the book of Luke.

Luke 6:12 states, "Now in those days it occurred that he went up into a mountain to pray and spent the whole night in prayer to God."

What's this? Jesus spent the whole night in prayer. He didn't pray just once and give up. He was persistent as he continually prayed to the Father. Jesus had been praying at the very worst time in his life, just before he was to be crucified. He knew the pain and suffering he would have to endure before heading to the cross. He was with his disciples in the book of Luke.

Luke 22:41–46 states, "And he withdrew from them about a stones throw and knelt down and prayed." (v. 41)

"Father if you are willing, remove this cup from me; yet not my will, but [always] yours be done." (v. 42)

"And there appeared to him an angel from heaven, strengthening him in spirit." (v. 43)

"And being in agony [of mind], he prayed all the more earnestly and intently, and his sweat became like great clots of blood dropping down upon the ground." (v. 44)

Jesus knows and understands what it's like to be in intense agony of mind!

JESUS KNOWS WHAT YOU ARE GOING THROUGH

For he endured every pain and temptation far above what you and I will ever have to endure, and he pressed through beyond his great, intense suffering because of his love for us and his obedience to God. He was able to do this through the power of prayer, and God answered him by sending an angel to give him strength. Now let's go back and read verse 45 and 46.

"And when he got up from prayer, he came to the disciples and found them sleeping from grief." (v. 45)

"And he said to them, 'Why do you sleep? Get up and pray that you may not enter [at all] into temptation." (v. 46)

As soon as Jesus was done praying, he immediately instructed his disciples to pray also as he knew the importance and power of prayer.

GOD GIVES US EXAMPLES OF THE POWER OF PRAYER

All the men and women of the Bible whom God has wrought his mighty works through were done through prayer! Let's look where an angel appeared to Daniel when he needed to interpret a vision.

Daniel 9:23 states, "At the beginning of your prayers, the word [giving an answer] went forth, and I have come to tell you for you are greatly beloved. Therefore, consider the matter and understand the vision" Now look down to Chapter 10.

Daniel 10:12 states, "Then he said to me [speaking of the angel that was talking to Daniel] Fear not Daniel, for from the first day that you set your heart and mind to understand and to humble yourself before your God, your words were heard, and I have come as a consequence of [and in response to] your words."

When Daniel prayed, God not only listened to his prayers, but also sent an angel to answer Daniel.

Interesting to see how God releases his angels to come help us in time of need when we pray.

ATTACKED FROM THE SOLE OF HIS FOOT TO THE CROWN OF HIS HEAD

Let's look at the story of Job when he was being severely attacked by the devil. His children and all his servants were killed, all his livestock taken away, even all his land and property were wiped out. As if this wasn't enough, Satan began attacking his health.

We read in Job 2:7, "So Satan went forth from the presence of the Lord and smote Job with loathsome and painful sores from the sole of his foot to the crown of his head."

Verse 12 tells us that Job was struck so severely that he was disfigured beyond recognition. Needless to say, Job had been attacked to the point where he dreaded the day he was born and wanted to die, as we read in chapter 3.

Even his own wife and friends were not obedient to God in helping Job. How alone Job must have felt during his affliction, and how many times do you feel alone when under attack? There are times in life where we don't understand why things happen, yet we still need to trust God for he has a purpose and a plan for us all. Job still remained faithful and never cursed God.

Job 42:1–2 "Then Job said to the Lord." (v. 1)

"I know you can do all things and that no thought or purpose of yours can be restrained or thwarted." (v. 2)

Then, look at verse 10. "And the Lord turned the captivity of Job and restored his fortunes when he prayed for his friends; also the Lord gave Job twice as much as he had before."

Even through all his tribulations, Job never gave up on prayer, and God turned everything around in Job's favor and blessed him when he prayed for his friends who were not obeying God.

GOD SEES OUR TEARS, HEARS OUR CRIES, AND ANSWERS OUR PRAYERS

Let's look at another example of prayer. It's in 1 Samuel chapter 1, where Elkanah had two wives: one, Hannah and the other, Peninnah. Peninnah had bore him children, but Hannah couldn't conceive. Every year, Elkanah would go to worship and make sacrifice to the Lord at a place called Shiloh. And on that day, he would give his wife, Peninnah, and her sons and daughters portions of the sacrificial meat. But to Hannah, his other wife, he gave a double portion, for he loved her even though the Lord had given her no children. This went on year after year and this embarrassed Hannah. Peninnah made fun of her and provoked her to make her cry and not eat because the Lord had left her childless.

Then, in 1 Samuel 1:9–20, we read, "So Hannah rose after they had eaten and drunk in Shiloh. Now, Eli, the priest, was sitting on his seat beside a post of the temple of the Lord." (v. 9)

"And Hannah was in distress of soul, praying to the Lord and weeping bitterly." (v. 10)

"She vowed, saying, 'O Lord of hosts, if you will indeed look on the affliction of your handmaid and [earnestly] remember, and not forget your handmaid but will give me a son, I will give him to the Lord all his life; no razor will touch his head.'" (v. 11)

"And as she continued praying before the Lord, Eli noticed her mouth." (v. 12)

"Hannah was speaking in her heart; only her lips moved but her voice was not heard. So Eli thought she was drunk." (v. 13)

"Eli said to her, 'How long will you be intoxicated? Put wine away from you.'" (v. 14)

"But Hannah answered, 'No, my lord, I am a woman of a sorrowful spirit. I have drunk neither wine nor strong drink, but I was pouring out my soul before the Lord.'" (v. 15)

This is what God desires that we do: pour out our hearts before him in prayer.

"Regard not your handmaid as a wicked woman; for out of my great complaint and bitter provocation I have been speaking." (v. 16)

Notice how Hannah didn't pray only once; she kept on praying to God.

"Then, Eli said, 'Go in peace and may the God of Israel grant your petition which you have asked of him.'" (v. 17)

"Hannah said, 'Let your handmaid find grace in your sight, so she went her way and ate, her countenance no longer sad.'" (v. 18)

Nothing in her situation had changed to this point except for the fact that she prayed to God, asking him for a son. Yet after her continual praying, she was no longer sad or in distress of mind and was able to eat because God had given her peace. *God can give you peace even in the midst of your trial before your prayers are answered.

"The family rose early the next morning, worshipped before the Lord, and returned to their home in Ramah. Elkanah knew Hannah, his wife [had intercourse with her], and the Lord remembered her." (v. 19)

Interesting to see how God wanted it noted here that they rose early and worshipped God and that the Lord remembered Hannah's prayer.

Now, in verse 20, "Hannah became pregnant and in due time, bore a son and named him Samuel [which means heard of God] because she said, 'I have asked him of the Lord.'"

GIVE GOD THE GLORY AND PRAISE

Then, in chapter 2, Hannah prays again, giving God the glory and praise.

1 Samuel 2:1, 2 and 4 states, "Hannah prayed, and said, 'My heart exults and triumphs in the Lord; my horn [my strength] is lifted up in the Lord. My mouth is no longer silent, for it is opened wide over my enemies because I rejoice in your salvation [web: deliverance from danger or difficulty]." (v. 1)

"There is none holy like the Lord, there is none besides you, there is no Rock like our God." (v. 2)

"The bows [web: to crush with a heavy burden] of the mighty [web: one possessing power] are broken and those who stumbled [web: to walk unsteadily] are girded [web: prepped for action] with strength [web: the power of resisting attack]." (v. 4)

Let's re-read this verse in its deeper meaning: The crushing heavy burdens of the one possessing power are broken (speaking of our enemy, Satan) and those who walked unsteadily are prepped for action with the power of resisting attack. Wow! What an amazing revelation God gives here when we pray.

LET'S PRAY!

The Battle Prayer

As I struggle, Lord, with this battle going on in my mind. I trust you to see me through. You are great, powerful, almighty, and worthy of my praise. I will seek your face in all I do. You never cease to amaze. Open up my eyes, Lord, to the wonders of your Word that I may bear witness of you in all the world. Give me strength to serve you with all my soul. I give you my life, your full control. Put the enemy beneath my feet, so I may glory in your name. Set me free from all attacks; let me never be the same. In the name above all names, through Jesus Christ, amen.

*This is a good prayer to write on your index cards and read every day before bed and first thing in the morning.

PRAYER MOVES THE HAND OF GOD

Do you want to see the hand of God in your life? Then, we must do as he instructs and PRAY! The devil will do anything he can to influence you not to pray. He may tell you lies such as the following:

- "Oh, God never answers my prayers like he does for other people."
- "I don't have time to pray."
- "Every time I pray, things seem to get worse."
- "I am not worthy to have things from God."
- "God is too busy to care about my needs."
- "My situation is hopeless."

The list goes on and on, but the bottom line is that these are all lies coming from the evil one; and this happens to be the first thing God instructs us to do each and every day. Does it mean that you won't go through trials or get attacked the day you pray? No, for Jesus said we will go through trials but when we pray, he promises to help us through them. When trials come, we only have two choices of what to do:

Complain, whimper, cower down, and let them defeat us trying to manage on our own which, by the way, is exactly what the enemy will try to persuade you to do so he can win and hurt you. Or...

Pray to our Lord God Almighty with humbleness, steadfastness, and as our vital necessity by leaning on the strength that he promises to provide, letting him fight the battle and see us through to victory.

There really is no other option, and I'm sure you, like me, find the second option to be more appealing. Thus, we need to make it a lifetime choice to do every day—before, during and after trials—and then you will start to see the hand of God move in your life.

Let's look now to an account of Elisha's days where we see how he did not give up on prayer until God came through, how God performed a great miracle in a very desperate time.

2 Kings 4:8–10 states, "One day, Elisha went on to Shunem where a rich and influential woman lived who insisted on his eating a meal. Afterward, whenever he passed by, he stopped there for a meal." (v. 8)

"And she said to her husband, Behold now, I perceive that this is a holy man of God who passes by continually." (v. 9)

"Let us make a small chamber on the [house top] and put there for him a bed, a table, a chair and a lamp. Then whenever he comes to us, he can go [up the outside stairs and rest] here." (v. 10)

Well, Elisha did just that and took up rest in the place where they prepared for him. Elisha was very grateful to the woman for how she chose to take care of him whenever he passed by and wanted to do something for her to bless her for her kindness as recorded in the next verses.

2 Kings 4:12–16 and 28 states, "And he said to Gehazi his servant, 'Call this Shunammite. When he had called her, she stood before him.'" (v. 12)

"And he said Gehazi, say now to her, 'You have been most painstakingly and reverently concerned for us, what is to be done for you? Would you like to be spoken for to the king or to the commander of the army?' She answered, 'I dwell among my own people [they are sufficient].'" (v. 13)

"Later Elisha said, 'What then is to be done for her?' Gehazi answered, 'She has no child and her husband is old.'" (v. 14)

"He said call her. Gehazi called her and she stood in the doorway." (v. 15)

"Elisha said, 'At this season when the time comes around, you shall embrace a son.' She said, 'No, my Lord, you man of God, do not lie to your housemaid.'" (v. 16)

Afterward, the woman did conceive a son that following season, just as Elisha had said. The child grew over the years and one day went out to his father in the field. All of a sudden, he began to complain of his head hurting so he was brought to his mother and laid upon her lap until he died. Here's where the attack of the enemy came to strike the woman, her family, and Elisha as well. But did Elisha cave? The mother took the child and laid him upon Elisha's bed and set out quickly where Elisha was. She came upon Elisha at Mt. Carmel and he could see she was upset and angry.

"Then she said, "Did I desire a son of my Lord? Did I not say, do not deceive me?" (v. 28)

Elisha, now realizing the child had died, instructed his servant to go on ahead of him and lay his staff upon the child's face, but the child still did not awaken or recover. Immediately, we see Elisha not cowering to the situation and accepting defeat, but instead acted out in prayer and faith by sending his servant on ahead to try to revive the child.

2 Kings 4:32–35 states, "When Elisha arrived in the house the child was dead and laid upon his bed." In verse 33, we see the key which released the great power of God.

"So he went in, shut the door on the two of them and prayed to the Lord." (v. 33) The first thing Elisha did was pray and then the Lord instructed him.

"He went up and lay on the child, Put his mouth on his mouth, his eyes on his eyes, and his hands on his hands. And as he stretched himself on him and embraced him, the child's flesh became warm." (v. 34)

"Then he returned and walked in the house to and fro and went up again and stretched himself upon him. And the child sneezed seven times and then opened his eyes." (v. 35)

In this account, we see a man of God going about doing God's business. He met a woman who blessed him along the way. And then, when tragedy stroke or the attack of the enemy befell both him and the woman, Elisha immediately looked to our Lord and prayed. Even though the boy did not rise up right away, Elisha still did not give in to fear, intimidation, or complaining but kept on praying, continually looking to God. He stretched himself upon the child, in faith, not once but twice as the Lord directed and the boy came back to life. Elisha had the Hand of God in his life through prayer.

How often do we pray and because we don't see results right away, we give up and reach out to worldly ways to seek help only to find ourselves now in bondage to them? Here, God is instructing us to pray and keep on praying until we see our desired result.

This reminds me of a time in my life that I have thought about over and over.

My father passed away back in August of 1992. He had a very bad heart condition and suffered many heart attacks. He was a great man who believed in God and taught me to believe in him as well. I can remember going to him at a very young age asking him about God and said, "How do you know there is a God?" My father answered back with two questions for me. He said, "Look around you, do you believe that someone had to make everything, that it couldn't have just appeared here in its own?" As I looked around at all the trees, sky, animals, etc., I agreed, yes! Then he asked the second question. "Do you believe that it had to be a supreme being, someone greater than us?" I quickly had to agree, "yes of course!" Then my father looked at me—and I will never forget the kindness or love he had in his eyes—and said, "That supreme being we call God!" Since that day, I've never doubted God's existence.

Well, my father passed away due to a major heart attack. He was living in Connecticut, and I was living in California when I got the news. I was completely heartbroken as we were very close. The next time I saw him, he was lying in a casket on the day of his wake. I was crying when I approached his casket, and I leaned over to hold his hand. I began to cry out to God while praying over my dad. Immediately, God's Word came to my mind—thoughts of how people were brought back to life from death—and I thought if God could do it then, He certainly could do it now. I began to pray that God would raise my father from the dead. As I began to pray, I felt my father's hand clench mine. Suddenly, I panicked and jumped away from the casket screaming out to everyone, "He moved!" The ushers from the funeral parlor quickly removed me and ushered me back to my seat. The thing that I have mulled over and over in my mind, to this day, is if I hadn't feared and just kept praying, would God have risen my father up from death, back to life? There is so much power in prayer, believer. We have to make the choice to

BELIEVE in the power of prayer. Satan will always att: with fear, but we can't let that intimidate or stop us.

DAVID PRAYS IN DEEP DISTRESS

David was obviously in deep distress as he was so many times in his life, constantly dealing with attacks of the enemy. Let's look now to an account where he writes in the book of Psalm.

Psalm 4:1 states, "Answer me when 1 call, O God of my righteousness [uprightness, justice and right standing with you]! You have freed me when I was hemmed [web: hemmed in by enemy troops, to fold back] in and enlarged [web: set free as captive] me when I was in distress [web: anguish of body or mind], have mercy upon me and hear my prayer."

During David's time of distress, he prayed to our Lord and asked God to answer him when he called and reminded God of his right standing with him. That's the first thing he did, then he recalled, in previous times of distress, how God delivered him and asked him to have mercy upon him once again.

I can remember many times while under attack, I would forget the previous times God was there and delivered me, and God reminded me to think on those times.

Satan would love for us to forget the things God has shown and done for us. We must keep reminding ourselves and ponder on all the wonderful things God has done for us and on what a faithful father he has been to you! Keep those things in the forefront of your mind and not the attack the enemy is presenting.

There are two verses of scripture that I suggest for you to write down and meditate on in the evening before bed and first thing in the morning.

Evening:

Psalm 4:8 states, "In peace, I will both lie down and sleep, for you, Lord, alone make me dwell in safety and confident trust."

In the evening, place yourself in God's care, and trust him to give you the rest you need, to be safe and that you remain in that confident trust that God provides.

Morning:

Psalm 5:3 states, "In the morning, you hear my voice, O Lord, in the morning I prepare [a prayer, a sacrifice] for you and watch and wait [for you to speak to my heart]."

In the morning, first thing upon waking, pray to God, your heavenly father. Talk to him and share all things as you would your best friend. God loves you and longs for us to have that close relationship with him. Then, wait and listen to him speak to your heart, and HE WILL!

Do not think that you are the only one or will be the last one the enemy tempts with this fear and panic. I can't stress enough how our forerunners had endured this great stress, pain, and struggle for God has addressed this very subject over and over in his Word.

HOW CAN WE RELATE TO DAVID?

David was feeling completely overwhelmed in body and mind, feeling a sense of total distress due to the attacks of the enemy. Sound familiar?

Psalm 6:1–10 states, "O Lord, rebuke [web: turn back or keep down] me not in your anger, nor discipline and chasten me in your hot displeasure." (v. 1)

"Have mercy [web: act of divine favor or compassion] on me and be gracious [web: marked by kindness or courtesy used conventionally of royalty and high nobility] to me, O Lord, for I am weak [web: faint and withered away]: O Lord, heal [web: to cause an undesirable condition to be overcome, return to a sound state] me, for my bones are troubled." (v. 2)

David prayed to the Lord in his deep distress, admitting his weakness, asking God to return him once again to a sound state. Why? Because David knew only God can do this, therefore making his plea.

"My [inner] self [as well as my body] is also exceedingly [web: darkness which surrounds a man's existence, to an extreme degree] disturbed [web: destroy the tranquility or composure of] and troubled [web: to agitate mentally or spiritually], But You O Lord, how long [until you return and speak peace to me]?" (v. 3)

I'm sure you can relate to David here as he shares with the Lord how he feels as he cries out in complete desperation, asking God how long until he (God) brings or restores him back to peace. David knew full well that only the Lord could give him peace during his attack. We all want that peace right away. But God has a plan and purpose, always in his time table; and he wants us to know that peace is indeed from him and that not from ourselves, so we may in turn give him the glory and praise!

"Return [web: restore to a normal or former state] [to my relief, O, Lord], deliver [web: set free from evil] my life. Save [web: rescue or deliver from danger or harm] me for the sake of your steadfast [web: not subject to change, immovable] love and mercy." (v. 4)

Here, David asked God to have him return to that sound peaceful state that he was in before the attack because of God's unchangeable love and mercy for him. David was fully aware of God's love and compassion for him, and we need to know and never doubt God's love and compassion for us as well. And because of that great love, he vows to rescue us every time.

"For in death, there is no remembrance of you; in Sheol [the place of the dead] who will give you thanks?" (v. 5)

I want you to think about this verse. David now spoke of death. He was being attacked so severely that he even feared that it could take his life if God didn't come to his aid. I too, can remember so many times being attacked so severely with fear and panic that I would cry out to God saying, "Either deliver me or let me die!"

"I am weary with my groaning; all night, I soak my pillow with tears. I drench my couch with my weeping." (v. 6)

Wow! David was really suffering here so much that it brought this man to his knees in tears! You are not alone in your tears, crying out to God.

"My eye [web: point of view] grows dim [web: having little prospect of a favorable result or outcome of the future] because of grief [web: trouble or annoyance]; it grows old because of all my enemies [web: adversary, a hostile unit or force]." (v. 7)

David recognized here that he knew full well what was going on and that it was due to all his enemies. Because of the trouble and annoying attacks from the enemy, it was causing him to lose perspective and was making him weaker. Then, after praying and asking God to help him in his desperate need, a surge of energy and strength came to David as he made a command to his attackers in the next verse.

"Depart from me, all you workers of iniquity [web: wickedness] for the Lord has heard the voice of my weeping." (v. 8)

How could David have gone from such a desperate state and then, with no apparent change in his situation, have risen with confidence and boldness, commanding his attackers to leave? The answer, believer, is through Prayer! God is showing you something here. It is through prayer that moves him, and the things that seemed so hopeless and impossible change and now become available through God. God had his Word [the Bible] written for our learning to help and aid us live this life while we are here in this world. We need to be obedient and adjust our lives to it if we want his hand working for us. If we truly want that freedom and peace that only he can give, we must change and adapt our thinking to think the Word. You may ask, "Well, how do I think the Word?" The only answer is to read, study, and put into application those things he instructs through his Word. How often? EVERY DAY!

"The Lord has heard my supplication [web: humble and earnest prayer]; the Lord receives my prayer." (v. 9)

David is telling us the Lord listens and receives our prayers.

"Let all my enemies be ashamed [web: feeling inferior or unworthy] and sorely troubled; let them turn back and be put to shame [web: condition of humiliating disgrace] suddenly." (v. 10)

Here, David asks that all his wicked attackers (Satan and his helpers) would feel a sense of inferiority next to our God as they run away now, feeling humiliated at the presence of our God and King. Amen, believer!

When we cry out to our God in prayer asking him to help us when the enemy attacks, *HE WILL*! That's it, He said it; and *HE WILL DO IT*! Don't let any devil in hell tell you different because it is contrary to what God says in his Word. Jesus already forewarned us not to listen to the devil because he is a *liar*! Jesus warned us of our enemy (Satan).

John 8:44b states, "He was a murderer from the beginning and does not stand in truth, because there is no truth in him, When he speaks a falsehood, he speaks what is natural to him for he is a liar [himself] and the father of lies and all that is false."

If you really want to be set free in your life, you must believe and trust what God himself is telling you through his Word, for his Word is truth.! Jesus prayed for us all.

John 17:17 states, "Sanctify them [purify, consecrate, separate them for yourself, make them holy] by truth: your Word is TRUTH."

Many things in this world will surely pass away, but God's Word will never pass away.

Isaiah 40:8 states, "The grass withers, the flower fades, but the Word of our God will stand forever."

Psalm 12:6 states, "The Words and promises of the Lord are pure [web: free from what makes faulty, defective, or weak] Words like silver refined in an earthen furnace, purified seven times over."

Think about this. How many things in this world are perfectly pure and will last forever? Not one! Except God's Holy Word. Therefore, we should make it of utmost importance to read, study, and obey it in order to obtain the knowledge that he shares within those words to live the life he desires for us all to have—one of LOVE, JOY, and FREEDOM!

GOD INSTRUCTS US TO PRAY IN THE FACE OF FEAR

What does God tell us to do when being attacked with fear? *PRAY*

In the book of Chronicles, there was a time when Jehoshaphat was king and the Moabites, Ammonites, and Menunites came against him to battle to take the land which God had given to him and his people. Suddenly, he became fearful. Let's read.

2 Chronicles 20:3–4 states, "Then Jehoshaphat feared and set himself [determinedly as his vital need] to seek the Lord, he proclaimed a fast in all Judah."

Here, we see when Jehoshaphat was afraid; he immediately sought God and instructed the people to do the same as we continue to read.

"And Judah gathered together to ask help from the Lord; even out of all the cities of Judah, they came to seek the Lord [yearning for him with all their desire]." (v. 4)

Here, we find the people seeking God with all their hearts. This is the way God wants us all to seek him, with our whole being. Then, Jehoshaphat prayed to God among the assembly.

2 Chronicles 20:6 states, "And said, O Lord, God of our fathers, are you not God in heaven? And do you not rule over all the Kingdoms of the nations? In your hand are power and might, so that none is able to withstand you."

This is an excellent prayer for you to write down and read during attacks from the enemy.

JEHOSHAPHAT REMINDS GOD

Then Jehoshaphat reminds God of his promise to give the land to Israel, descendants of Abraham [God's friend], and how they continued to worship him, building a sanctuary in God's name. And when Israel came out of Egypt and came upon the land of Ammon, Moab, and Mount Seir, you told us not to destroy them but look now at what they are doing in trying to overtake us.

2 Chronicles 20:11 states, "Behold, they reward us by coming to drive us out of your possession which you have given us to inherit."

How many times in your own life do you see the same people you help or bless come back and allow the enemy to attack you through them? This is nothing new, and the same believers throughout history have endured these same trials.

JEHOSHAPHAT CONCLUDES HIS PRAYER

2 Chronicles 20:12 states, "O our God, will you not exercise judgment upon them? For we have no might to stand against this great company that is coming against us. We do not know what to do but our eyes are upon you."

Another good prayer to write down in the midst of Satan's attacks!

How many times do you also feel helpless when the intimidation of Satan knocks at your door with fear and panic, not knowing what to do? I know for myself when Satan would come to me with blazing guns, attacking me to the core of my being, I felt so helpless like a spineless coward. I had always considered myself to be a pretty strong person, thinking I could handle anything that came my way. But later, God would teach me that this was my own pride and that I would need to be brought down to my knees before I would realize that his will was for me to live by his strength and not my own.

Like what Jehoshaphat said in the latter part of this verse, we don't know what to do, *but* our eyes are upon you. He humbled himself before the Lord.

GODS SPEAKS AND GIVES INSTRUCTION

Now, as we read on, after Jehoshaphat and the people of Judah had prayed to the Lord, God spoke to them through Jahaziel in the midst of the assembly.

2 Chronicles 20:14–25 states, "Then the spirit of the Lord came upon Jahaziel, son of Zechariah, the son of Benaiah, the son of Jeiel, the son of Mattaniah, a Levite of the sons of Asaph, in the midst of the assembly. (v. 14)

"He said, Harken all Judah, you inhabitants of Jerusalem! And you, king Jehoshaphat, The Lord says this to you: Be not afraid or dismayed [web: sudden loss of courage through the pressure of sudden fear, anxiety, or great perplexity] at this great multitude: for the battle is not yours but God's." (v. 15)

What's this? God is telling them not to be afraid that the battle is not theirs to fight or contend with, but it is *his* battle. *Remember, we are all in a spiritual battle, one that cannot be fought in our own human strength but only through and with the power of God. God answers their prayers by speaking through one of their own people and instructs them what to do.

"Tomorrow, go down to them. Behold, they will come up by the ascent of Ziz and you will find them at the end of the ravine [web: small, narrow, steep-sided valley] before the wilderness of Jeruel." (v. 16)

It is very interesting to see how, when God began to give them instruction of what to do, he didn't say wait or hold back. He actually told the people to go down to them and let them know ahead of time where their enemies or the armies would be. God does not want us to hold back or run from fear but rather face it head on knowing *HE IS WITH US!*

"You shall not need to fight in this battle; take your positions, stand still and see the deliverance of the Lord [who is] with you, O Judah and Jerusalem. Fear not nor be dismayed [web: to deprive of courage and initiative through the pressure of sudden fear or anxiety of great perplexities or difficulties]. Tomorrow, go out against them, for the Lord is with you." (v. 17)

GIVING GOD GLORY AND PRAISE

It is very important during battles to give God glory and praise! Even though it doesn't make sense to our own human thinking, this is what the Lord instructs. Therefore, we need to be obedient to the examples he shows us through his Word and simply just do it whole-heartedly if we want to live a victorious life.

"And Jehoshaphat bowed his head with his face to the ground, and all Judah and inhabitants of Jerusalem fell down before the Lord worshiping him." (v. 18)

"And some Levites of the Kohathites and Korahites stood up to praise the Lord, the God of Israel with a very loud voice." (v. 19)

When under attack, speak out loud over your situation, claiming God's Word and his promises and giving God all the glory and praise. The word *praise*, according to *Webster*, means to say or write good things about someone, to express thanks to or love and respect in this case for God.

"And they rose early in the morning and went out into the wilderness of Tekoa, and as they went out, Jehoshaphat stood and said, Hear me, O Judah, and you inhabitants of Jerusalem, Believe in the Lord your God and you shall be established [web: make firm or stable]; believe and remain steadfast [web: firm in belief] to his prophets, and you shall prosper." (v. 20)

Jehoshaphat tells the people to believe in the Lord without doubting and they shall see success.

GIVING THANKS BEFORE DELIVERANCE

"When he had consulted with the people, he appointed singers to sing to the Lord and praise him in their holy garments as they went out before the army saying, 'Give thanks to the Lord for his mercy and loving kindness endure forever!'" (v. 21)

Not only did King Jehoshaphat and the people give thanks and sing praises to the Lord, but also as they went out, they were giving God thanks as if they already had the victory.

THE VICTORY

"And when they began to sing and to praise, The Lord set ambushments [web: traps in which concealed persons who lie in wait to attack by surprise] against the men of Ammon, Moab, and Mount Seir who had come against Judah and they were self slaughtered." (v. 22)

All the men who came to battle against Jehoshaphat and God's people started distrusting each other, therefore killing one another. Just as Satan can and does present thoughts to our minds, so can our God present thoughts to the minds of people to benefit his plans. In the next verse, we see why their enemy turned on one another.

"For [suspecting betrayal] the men of Ammon and Moab rose against those of Mount Seir, utterly destroying them. And when they had made an end of the men of Mount Seir they all helped to destroy one another." (v. 23)

"And when Judah came to the watch tower of the wilderness, they looked at the multitude and behold, they were dead bodies fallen to the earth and none had escaped." (v. 24)

Wow When you pray to God and seek him as your vital need, *HE WILL* help you and will leave no stone unturned!

GOD'S PROMISE TO REWARD

When you follow God's instructions as set forth in his Word and are obedient to do them, he not only delivers from the trials or attacks from the enemy (Satan) but afterward, because of our faithfulness, he promises to reward us. He did the same for King Jehoshaphat and the people of Judah as we find in the next verse.

"When Jehoshaphat and his people came to take the spoil [web: something gained by a special effort] they found among them much cattle, goods, garments, and precious things which they took for themselves, more than they could carry. So much they were three days in gathering the spoil." (v. 25)

Here, God gives an example of what he did for our learning. Not only did God deliver them as he promised when they prayed and diligently sought him out as their vital necessity, but he also rewarded them for their troubles and obedience. He promises to do the same for us when we follow his instructions as well.

Hebrews 11:6b states, "Believe that God exists and that he is the rewarder of those who earnestly and diligently seek him [out]."

Zechariah 9:12 states, "Return to the stronghold [of security and prosperity] you prisoners of hope; even today do I declare, I will restore double your former prosperity to you."

Isaiah 61:7 states, "Instead of your former shame [web: condition of humiliating disgrace] you shall have a twofold recompense [web: a return for something suffered]; instead of dishonor and reproach [web: a cause or occasion of blame], your people shall rejoice in their portion. Therefore in all their land, they shall possess double [what they had forefeited]; everlasting joy shall be theirs." This is what I call a win-win situation—when we pray and follow Gods instructions that he reveals to us as we read and study his Word!

So beloved believer, if you want to see the hand of our Almighty God in your life, know that God instructs you to pray. How often should we pray? Continually!

Ephesians 6:18a states, "Pray at all times, [on every occasion, in every season] in the Spirit with all [manner of] prayer and entreaty [web: to plead or ask for urgently]."

And when you do pray, God promises that he not only will listen, but will also answer us and give us instruction of what to do.

Psalm 32:8 states, "I [the Lord] will instruct you and teach you in the way you should go; I will council you with my eye upon you."

Amen!

Chapter
3

Be Mindful of Your Thoughts

SATAN PRESENTS LIES TO OUR MINDS

The first place Satan will come with his attack is through your thought process. I've heard people say, "Give him one thought, and he'll take your whole head."

Jesus tells us in John 10:10, "The thief (Satan) comes only in order to steal, kill, and destroy. I came that they may have and enjoy life and have it in abundance [to the fullest, till it overflows]."

Satan knows if he can stop you, keep you frozen in fear, then he can stop the movement of God here on this earth. This is his main goal. The battle is and always was between him and God, and in the end of this system, the great battle will be fought.

Revelation 19:14 and 19 states, "And the troops of heaven, clothed in fine linen, dazzling and clean, followed him on white horses." (v. 14)

"Then, I saw the beast (Satan) and the rulers and leaders of the earth with their troops mustered to go into battle and make war against him who is mounted on the horse (Jesus) and against his troops." (v. 19)

In the end Satan does ultimately lose this battle as we read in verse 20 "and the beast was seized and overpowered and with him the false prophet who in his presence had worked wonders and performed miracles by which he led astray those who had accepted or permitted to be placed upon them the stamp (mark) of the beast and those who paid homage and gave divine honors to his statue. Both of them were hurled alive into the fiery lake that burns and blazes with brimstone."

*Until this great battle is to be fought at the end of this system we need to adhere to what God's Word says and be compliant in following his instructions. He (God) does not want to see us getting fooled or tricked by the enemy (Satan) no, not even for a moment...

YOU ARE A CHILD OF GOD

When you come to accept God in your life, you have also joined forces with him and are now a child of the living God. As a child of God, you need not fear Satan nor his attacks.

1 John 4:4 and 6 states, "Little children, you are of God [you belong to him] and have [already] defeated and overcome them [the agents of the anti-Christ] because he who lives in you is greater [mightier] than he who is in the world. (v. 4)

"We are [children] of God. Whoever is learning to know God [progressively to perceive, recognize, and understand God by observation and experience and to get an ever clearer knowledge of him] listens to us, and he who is not of God does not listen or pay attention to us. By this we know [recognize] the Spirit of truth and the Spirit of error." (v. 6)

Therefore, Satan hates you and I with a cruel hatred. Don't wonder why you keep getting attacked by him. He is very cunning, crafty, and all about deception through trickery. If he can get you to believe him (his lies) instead of God's Word (which is truth), then he's won.

GOD CAN DELIVER

When I was first being hit with fear and panic, I prayed to God and screamed at the devil. I asked God to please show me what to do. He led me to the book of Psalms.

Psalm 34:4 states, "I sought [inquired] of the Lord and required him [of necessity and on the authority of his Word] and he heard me and delivered me from all my fears."

Notice that God says here "all my fears" not just some. The word *delivered* here means to set free, come through on his promise, or rescue. Obviously, God knew we would be attacked with fear; otherwise, we would not need deliverance from it. All over the Word, God tells us to "Fear Not"! I know when your whole body is under attack and in a state of anxiety, panic, and trembling, it's hard to fear not. God knows this too for there is nothing in this world that he does not understand, have compassion and the willingness to rescue US, his children from. That's why he gives us his Word, for it's in his Word that we find true freedom. We must come to the understanding of how vitally important it is for us to seek out answers from God through his Word.

SATAN INTRODUCES DOUBT

Let's look from the very beginning of man in Genesis chapter 2. Adam and Eve were living blissfully in perfect harmony and fellowship with the Lord. Everything was beautiful with no sickness, death, or misery. They were filled with peace, joy, and everything they needed in abundance, lacking nothing. They were completely unaware of any evil. Let's read the account.

Genesis 2:8 and 9 states, "And the Lord planted a garden toward the East in Eden [delight] and there, he put the man [Adam] whom he had formed." (v. 8)

"And out of the ground, the Lord made to grow every tree that is pleasant to the sight or to be desired good [suitable, pleasant] for food, the tree of life also in the center of the garden and the tree of knowledge of good and evil [the difference between good and evil and blessing and calamity]." (v. 9)

GOD SPEAKS TRUTH

Genesis 2:16 and 17 states, "And the Lord commanded saying, 'You may freely eat of every tree of the garden.'" (v. 16)

"But of the tree of knowledge of good and evil and blessing and calamity, you shall not eat, for in the day that you eat of it, you shall surely die." (v. 17)

These were words of truth that God spoke to Adam. God never wanted us to know evil or calamity.

SATAN PRESENTS DOUBT

Genesis 3:1–3 states, "Now the serpent was more subtle and crafty [web: clever, adept in the use of subtlety and cunning) than any living creature of the field which the Lord God had made. And he (Satan) said to the woman, can it really be that God has said, you shall not eat from every tree of the garden?" (v. 1)

Satan presented the question to Eve here to doubt the Word of God and continues to do this to us even in this present day.

"And the woman said to the serpent, 'We may eat of the fruit of the trees of the garden.'" (v. 2)

"Except the fruit from the tree which is in the middle of the garden, God has said, 'You shall not eat of it, neither shall you touch it, lest you die.'" (v. 3)

Eve basically tells the devil what God has said.

SATAN INTRODUCES HIS LIE

Genesis 3:4–5 states, "But the serpent said to the woman. You shall not surely die." (v. 4)

Here, we find the first lie ever recorded, where the devil calls God a liar trying to persuade Eve that what *he* says is truth.

"For God knows that in the day you eat of it your eyes will be opened, and you will be like God, knowing the difference between good and evil and blessing and calamity." (v. 5)

EVE BELIEVES THE LIE AND ACTS UPON IT

Genesis 3:6 states, "And when the woman saw that the tree was good [suitable and pleasant] for food and that it was delightful to look at, and a tree to be desired in order to make one wise, she took of its fruit and ate and she gave some also to her husband and he ate."

Afterward, Eve realizes she was deceived and tricked by the devil.

Genesis 3:13 states, "And the Lord God said to the woman, 'What is this you have done?' And the woman said, 'The serpent beguiled [web: cheated, outwitted and deceived] me and I ate.

Satan is using these very same strategies today. He is preying on those not fully knowing, understanding, or believing God's Word (Bible) to overtake us in his attacks. If you want to be delivered from the attacks of fear and panic, you must first realize where the attacks are coming from and go to the only source of complete freedom, which God offers through his Word.

GOD IS YOUR FATHER

Satan will try to deceive you into thinking something's wrong with you but on the contrary, it's because something's right with you. You belong to God, and therefore, he is your Father.

Romans 8:14–16 states, "For all who are led by the spirit of God are sons of God." (v. 14)

"For [the spirit which] you have now received [is] not a spirit of slavery to put you once more in bondage to fear, but you have received the Spirit of adoption [the spirit producing sonship] in which we cry abba Father." (v. 15)

"The spirit himself testifies together with our own spirit [assuring us] that we are the children of God." (v. 16)

NOT WHAT GOD INTENDED

Later on, in Genesis 6, we find there was great evil upon the earth and much suffering. Things were no longer peaceful or joyous and man's connection/fellowship with God was greatly hindered. This was never God's intent for us to suffer and live among evil. He regretted that he even created man to begin with.

Genesis 6:5 and 6 states, "The Lord saw that the wickedness of man was great in all the earth and that every imagination and intention of all human thinking was only evil continually." (v. 5)

"And the Lord regretted that he had made man on the earth and was grieved at heart." (v. 6)

Interesting here how God speaks of all human thinking. He doesn't mention doing because he knows thinking precedes doing.

WANDERING THOUGHTS

In the book of Chronicles, David the king speaks to Solomon his son about wandering thoughts.

1 Chronicles 28:9a states, "And you, Solomon, my son know the God of your father [have personal knowledge of him, be acquainted with and understand him, appreciate, need and cherish him] and serve him with a blameless heart and a willing mind. For the Lord searches all the hearts and minds and understands all the wanderings of the thoughts. If you seek him [inquiring for and of him and requiring him as your first and vital necessity], you will find him."

Here, God is telling us he understands our thoughts tend to wander, and he is also telling us what to do when they do. Seek him first as your vital necessity. Vital here means of the utmost importance, essential to continued worth or well-being.

GOD CAN ESTABLISH OUR THOUGHTS

Then in chapter 29, David prays to God to keep godly thoughts in the minds of his people.

1 Chronicles 29:18 states, "O Lord God of Abraham, Isaac and Israel, our fathers, keep forever such purposes and thoughts in the minds of your people and direct and establish their hearts toward you."

Satan can and does try to hinder or influence our thoughts into his way of thinking. Thoughts of fear, panic, worry, and anxiety are just a few that he hits our minds with. God can and will establish our thoughts in right thinking and doing.

Proverbs 16:3 states, "Commit thy works unto the Lord, and thy thoughts shall be established." (KJV) Established means to make stable, set on a firm basis, or put beyond doubt.

Proverbs 16:3 states, "Roll your works upon the Lord [commit and trust them wholly to him, and he will cause your thoughts to become agreeable to his will] so shall your plans be established and succeed." (AMP)

Proverbs 15:15 states, "All the days of the desponding and afflicted are made evil [by anxious thoughts and forebodings] but he who has a glad heart has a continual feast [regardless of circumstances]."

Let's do a word study on this verse for its clearer and deeper meaning. *Webster* defines the following terms:

• Desponding—feeling extreme discouragement or depression over ones health

- Afflicted—to distress so severely as to cause persistent suffering or anguish
- Evil—causing discomfort, harm, or institution of slavery
- Anxious—uneasiness of mind or brooding fear
- Forebodings—having an inward conviction of becoming ill or misfortune
- Glad—very willing to do it (Note: The King James Version uses the word *merry* instead of *glad*, which means praised.)
- Feast—something that gives unusual or abundant pleasure

Now, let's re-read this verse in its deeper meaning to give better understanding and clarity.

This is the paraphrased version of Proverbs 15:15: All the days of the one feeling extreme discouragement or depression over ones health and the one distressed so severely causing persistent suffering are made to cause discomfort and become enslaved by uneasiness of mind or brooding fearful thoughts and having an inward conviction of becoming ill or having misfortune, but he who has a willing or praiseful heart has continual abundant pleasure.

God wants us to have a willing and praiseful heart regardless of circumstances—a willingness to move forward in the face of fear and to praise him before, during, and after our trials. He tells us to seek him as our vital necessity, putting our complete trust in him to see us through anything that tries to hinder, harm, or stop us from having the continual abundant pleasure he desires for us all to have.

As we live in this world, God never intended for us to have our thoughts wander. This is only an open door to invite Satan to fill our thoughts and minds with his lies, evil, and everything that sets itself up against the true knowledge of God.

2 Corinthians 10:5 states, "[Inasmuch as we] refute arguments, theories, and reasonings and every proud and lofty thing that sets itself up against the [true] knowledge of God, and we lead every thought and purpose captive into the obedience of Christ (the Messiah, the Anointed One)."

And how we lead every thought captive is to replace every thought with thoughts of the Word! Remember, Satan's main goal is to steal, kill, and destroy us all because of his rebellion and hatred toward God. God's desire is for us to know and think the Word, which is truth that leads to life, joy, and happiness.

The only way to receive the complete freedom that God desires for us all to have is by having a close-knit relationship with him. The only way to have this close relationship with him is through prayer (conversing with him daily) and the constant, continual studying and reading of his Word of Truth. How can the truth set you free if you don't know it?

THOUGHTS OF THE MIND

Let's look at a few more verses of scripture where God speaks of thoughts of the mind.

Isaiah 55:8 and 9 states, "For my thoughts are not your thoughts, neither are your ways, My ways, says the Lord." (v. 8)

Because of Adam and Eve's disobedience from the very beginning of this world, eating of the tree of knowledge of good and evil, we are all now exposed to evil thoughts or evil thinking. God never wanted our minds to be opened to these things, allowing Satan the enemy to come into our minds. This is why in this verse, God says our thoughts and ways are not his ways. The God we serve is all good, and there is no evil in him.

"For as the heavens are higher than the earth, so are My ways higher than your ways and My thoughts than your thoughts." (v. 9)

The word *higher* here, according to *Webster*, means "exulted in character, noble." In the book of Ezekiel, God speaks of evil thoughts coming into the mind of the prince of Rosh through the prophet Ezekiel, whose name means "God is strong". Ezekiel prophesied as the Lord commanded him, speaking of Israel in the book of Ezekiel.

Ezekiel 37:26–28 states, "I will make a covenant of peace with them; it shall be an everlasting covenant with them, and I will give blessings to them and multiply them and will set my sanctuary [web: place of worship, refuge, and protection] in the midst of them forevermore." (v. 26)

"My tabernacle or dwelling place also shall be with them, and I will be their God and they shall be my people." (v. 27)

"Then, the nations shall know, understand, and realize that I, the Lord, do set apart and consecrate Israel for holy use, when my sanctuary shall be in their midst forevermore." (v. 28)

*Note: Of every place in this earth, God chose Israel to be a Holy Land therefore we should always support Israel.

Then the Lord spoke to Ezekiel concerning a man called Gog, the prince of Rosh, saying he was against him because he knew Gog would be planning to attack Israel as we continue reading.

Ezekiel 38:10 states, "Thus says the Lord God; at the same time, thoughts shall come into your mind and you will devise a plan."

God knows our thoughts ahead of time and knows evil thoughts precede action. In this case, the evil thoughts were that of destruction to Israel through the mind of Gog. On the other hand, evil thoughts can be that of fear, doubt, panic, anxiety, sickness, etc. This is where it all starts—with a thought presented to our minds. We choose whether to act out on that thought. God instructs that we replace all negative or evil thoughts that come to mind which Satan presents with positive thoughts of the Word! And if we obey and do this, God promises to deliver us, bringing us peace, stability, love, and God's joy!

You may be telling yourself, "Well, this is hard to do, I can't help dwelling on the thoughts that come into my mind." Well, know, believer, this is another lie coming straight from the pit of hell. You *CAN* stop dwelling on each and every thought that comes into your mind with God's help. We can't stop the evil thoughts presented to our minds, but you choose whether to entertain or dwell on those thoughts. God would never ask us to do something that we could not do, and when we choose to obey God and do those things he instructs, he also promises to help us every step of the way. This is key to your release!

After years of entertaining these negative thoughts, your mind has been trained, so to speak, and has created habit patterns that your mind automatically follows. But as you begin the process of changing your mind to think the Word, you will start to retrain your mind to dwell on right thoughts of the Word, bringing you out of captivity; and the fruits of joy, success, and freedom will be yours.

When God had first started showing me these very things, he gave me this analogy:

You have two glasses of water: one is dirty water, and one is clean water. The glass is your mind. The dirty water represents Satan and all his lies, and the clean water represents God and his Holy Word.

Your Mind

Dirty Water

Satan's Lies and the filth he presents.

Clean Water

Gods Word Holy and Pure.

As you begin to pour the Truths of Gods Word into your mind, it begins to filter out all the impurities Satan has built up for years and eventually your mind thinks pure thoughts of the Word.

As you begin to slowly pour the pure/clean water into the glass of dirty water, the dirty water eventually becomes pure and clean as it filters out all the impurities. This takes time and doesn't happen in an instant. Likewise, this is true of our minds. Therefore, we must start doing as God instructs and be patient. Just as it took years for your mind to be conditioned to bring you into the state you're in, it will take time for it to be re-conditioned to have it restored to the way God intends, bringing the victorious life that he desires for us all to have. Another thing I might add here, believer, is that the more time you spend with the Lord and studying the Word, the quicker the process.

You do have a choice. You choose.

MAKING RIGHT CHOICES

In the book of Daniel, we find three men of God who, after evil was presented to their minds, even to the point where they feared for their lives, they still made the right choice to obey God and adhere to his Word; and God delivered them. We find the account in Daniel chapter 3 where there reigned a king called Nebuchadnezzar. He constructed an image of gold and upon completion, he commanded that every time the people heard music they needed to fall down and worship the golden image that he had made.

Daniel 3:4 and 5 states, "Then the herald cried aloud, You are commanded, O peoples, nations, and languages." (v. 4)

"That when you hear the sound of the horn, pipe, lyre [web: a harped like instrument], trigon [web: an ancient triangular harp], harp, dulcimer [web: stringed instrument] or bagpipe and every kind of music, you are to fall down and worship the golden image that king Nebuchadnezzar has set up." (v. 5)

Now, we have to recognize who was ultimately behind this act. It was indeed the enemy, Satan, working through the king to command the people to disobey God.

Then, he uses intimidation to place fear in the thoughts and minds of the people if they refused to obey as found in the next verse.

Daniel 3:6 states, "And whoever does not fall down and worship shall that very hour be cast into the midst of a burning fiery furnace."

The people, after considering the thought presented to their minds, did as the king commanded even though God specifically warned against worshiping other gods—all, except for three men named Shadrach, Meshach, and Abednego. This angered the king, and he confronted these three men.

Daniel 3:14 and 15 state, "[Then] Nebuchadnezzar said to them, 'Is it true, O Shadrach, Meshach, and Abednego, that you do not serve my gods or worship the golden image which I have set up?'"

Then the king intimidates them with fear to obey his command and disobey God.

"Now, if you are ready, when you hear the sound of the horn, pipe, lyre, trigon, harp, dulcimer or bagpipe and every kind of music, to fall down and worship the image which I have made, very good; But if you do not worship, you shall be cast at once into the midst of a burning fiery furnace, and who is that god who can deliver you out of my hands?" (v. 15)

Even though it is the king presenting these things to these three men, we have to recognize ultimately who is working behind the scenes here through King Nebuchadnezzar to get them to disobey God. It is our enemy, Satan! Satan can and will work through people if they allow to get us to stray from God and his will.

Shadrach, Meshach, and Abednego did not let the intimidation of the enemy cause them to disobey but did as the Lord commands, and that is to trust in God even in the midst of the storm or frightening circumstances.

Daniel 3:17 and 18 states, "If our God whom we serve is able to deliver us from the burning fiery furnace, he will deliver us out of your hand, O King!" (v. 17)

"But if not, let it be known to you; O King, that we will not serve your gods or worship the golden image which was set up." (v. 18)

SATAN'S RAGE

When we choose to obey God in the midst of battles, this infuriates Satan, and he will try to pump up the volume, so to speak, and set up even worse circumstances for us to bear.

This is where many of us fail. Many times after praying, we find circumstances now to get worse than before we prayed and therefore give up on prayer and give in to the circumstance. Don't be fooled by him and recognize where its coming from and still trust in God as did these three men who God had recorded here for our learning. Satan's rage works through king Nebuchadnezar.

Daniel 3:19–21 states, "Then Nebuchadnezzar was full of fury and his facial expression was changed [to antagonism] [web: hostility] against Shadrach, Meshach, and Abednego, therefore he commanded that the furnace should be heated seven times hotter than it was usually heated." (v. 19)

How many times during your trials, do you see your circumstance change for the worse?

Well, this was the case for these men and that's the time we need to keep pressing through, not taking our eyes or focus off God for a second. God is speaking to us all here as to why this happens and is telling us that as we continue to persevere, he will bring us out victoriously as he did for Shadrach, Meshach, and Abednego.

"And he commanded the strongest men in his army to bind Shadrach, Meshach, and Abednego and to cast them into the burning fiery furnace." (v. 20)

"Then these [three] men were bound in their cloaks, their tunics or undergarments, their turbans and their other clothing and they were cast into the midst of the burning fiery furnace." (v. 21)

OBEDIENCE AND TRUST BRINGS VICTORY

Even through these grave circumstances that even seemed fatal, Shadrach, Meshach, and Abednego did not waiver. Because our God is a faithful God and is true to his Word (one who can be trusted), God delivered these men by fighting for them in a most miraculous way and brought victory over the enemy as we continue to read.

Daniel 3:22–25 states, "Therefore, because the king's commandment was urgent and the furnace exceedingly hot, the flame and sparks from the fire killed those men who handled Shadrach, Meshach, and Abednego." (v. 22)

"And these three men, Shadrach, Meshach, and Abednego, fell down bound into the burning fiery furnace." (v. 23)

"Then, Nebuchadnezzar the king [saw and] was astounded and he jumped up and said to his counselors, 'Did we not cast three men bound into the midst of the fire? They answered, 'True, O King.'" (v. 24)

"He answered, 'Behold, I see four men loose, walking in the midst of the fire, and they are not hurt! And the form of the forth is like a son of the gods!" (v. 25)

God can do the impossible and rescue us from the hand of the enemy if we press through, trust, believe, and obey during battles!

God can and will deliver us from the enemies' attacks if we follow his instructions set forth in his Word as he did for these three men. He also sent them help, talking about the forth form who appeared in the furnace with them.

GOD BLESSES BEYOND OUR IMAGINATION

Not only did God deliver these three men out of the hand of the enemy, but he also did it in such a way that there was no way to misconstrue that it was indeed by the hand of God and that it was inconceivable to our minds or five senses. What an awesome God we serve, and he has all power and might whose resources are limitless. Let's continue to read the miraculous account.

Daniel 3:26–30 states, "Then, Nebuchadnezzar came near to the mouth of the burning fiery furnace and said Shadrach, Meshach, and Abednego, you servants of the most High God, come out and come here. Then Shadrach, Meshach, and Abednego came out from the midst of the fire." (v. 26)

"And the satraps [web: governor of ancient Persia], the deputies, the governors, and the king's counselors gathered around together and saw these men that the fire had no power upon their bodies, nor was the hair of their head singed, neither was their garments scorched or changed in color or condition, nor had even the smell of smoke clung to them." (v. 27)

Wow, believer, only our God can deliver in this way. As if they weren't affected by the fire in any way at all! If he can deliver these men in such a miraculous way, then he can certainly deliver you! Not only did God deliver these men, but he made a believer out of the king as well; and what a witness it was to everyone else there.

"Then, Nebuchadnezzar said, 'Blessed be the God of Shadrach, Meshach, and Abednego, who has sent his angel and delivered his servants who believe in, trusted in, and relied on him! And they set aside the kings command and yielded their bodies rather than serve or worship any god except their own God." (v. 28)

In this verse, we find three important keys God had recorded here for our learning that precedes deliverance:

1. Believe in God.
2. Trust in God.
3. Rely on God.

Then, the king made a statement or order.

"Therefore, I will make a decree, that any people, nation, and language that speaks anything amiss against the God of Shadrach, Meshach, and Abednego shall be cut in pieces and their houses be made a dunghill [web: heap of manure] for there is no other God who can deliver in this way." (v. 29)

"Then, the king promoted Shadrach, Meshach, and Abednego in the province of Babylon." (v. 30)

Here, we find that by these three men's obedience to God, that he (God) not only delivered them, but he also rewarded them by promoting them in the kingdom. We will read more about how God rewards obedience later in this study.

In conclusion, who will help you in your time of need against the enemy in his attacks of anxious thoughts? Yes! Our God says *HE WILL* and promises to do so every time.

Psalm 94:16–19 states, "Who will rise up for me against the evil doers? Who will stand up for me against the workers of iniquity [web: wickedness]?" (v. 16)

"Unless the Lord had been my help, I would soon have dwelt in [the land where there is] silence." (v. 17)

"When I said, 'My foot is slipping,' Your mercy and loving kindness, O Lord, held me up." (v. 18)

"In the multitude [web: the state of many] of my anxious thoughts within me, your comforts [web: consolation in time of trouble or worry] cheer [web: instill with hope or courage] and delight (web: give joy or satisfaction) my soul." (v. 19)

Let's re-read this verse for more clarity: In the state of many of my anxious thoughts within me, your consolation in times of trouble or worry instill within me hope or courage and give joy or satisfaction to my inner self.

Chapter
4

We Are In A Spiritual Battle

Satan relentlessly tries to manipulate and build strongholds in our minds, putting us in bondage to our thoughts, fears, anxieties, and worries.

2 Corinthians 11:3 states, "But [now], I am fearful, lest that even as the serpent beguiled [web: led by deception, persuaded by use of tricks intended to ensnare or deceive] Eve by his cunning [web: characterized by wiliness and trickery, prettily appealing], so your minds may be corrupted [web: to alter from the original or correct form or version, to become tainted or rotten] and seduced [web: persuade to disobedience or disloyalty, lead astray by persuasion or false promises] from whole hearted and sincere and pure devotion to Christ."

Satan has studied us for many years and has a very calculated strategy and plan to destroy us! When are we going to believe what the Word says?

Every day we are in a spiritual battle and make decisions to believe what the Word says or believe what the devil presents to our minds. We need to make the decision to believe what the Words says and do those things that God instructs in order to gain that peace, understanding, and blessings that he desires for us all to have.

GOD'S WORD IS OUR WEAPON

2 Corinthians 10:3–5 states, "For though we walk [live] in the flesh, we are not carrying on our warfare according to the flesh and using mere human weapons." (v. 3)

God is telling us here that *WE ARE IN A WAR*—one that cannot be fought using mere human weapons!

"For the weapons of our warfare are not physical [weapons of flesh and blood], but they are mighty before God for the overthrow and destruction of strongholds." (v. 4)

A stronghold is a mentally strong place.

If we are not in a spiritual battle, then why does God say here "weapons of our warfare"? He wants us to know that we are in a spiritual battle! Spiritual battle against who? Our enemy, the devil!

"[Inasmuch as we] refute [web: show to be false] arguments and theories and reasonings and every proud and lofty thing that sets itself up against the [true] knowledge of God and we lead every thought and purpose away captive into the obedience of Christ [the Messiah, the Anointed One]." (v. 5)

What are our weapons, then, if not flesh and blood or physical weapons? God tells us in his Word.

Proverbs 30:5 states, "Every Word of God is pure; he is a shield unto them that put their trust in him." (KJV)

Psalm 18:30 states, "As for God, his way is perfect! The Word of the Lord is tested and tried; He is a shield to all those who take refuge and put their trust in him."

Psalm 115:9 states, "O Israel, trust and take refuge in the Lord; [lean on, rely on, and be confident in him!]. He is their help and their shield." Here we find in the Word, God speaks of his Word being our shield.

Now let's look into the book of Ephesians where God mentions more of our spirit armor and what we are instructed to do during attacks of the devil.

Ephesians 6:10 and 11 states, "In conclusion, be strong [web: having or marked by great physical power] in the Lord [be empowered through your union with him], draw your strength from him, [that strength which his boundless might provides]." (v. 10)

The only way to be strong in the Lord is to have union (web: formation of an independent unit, coming together as one) with him, and God's strength is boundless (without limits).

"Put on God's whole armor [the armor of a heavy armed soldier which God supplies] that you may be able successfully to stand up against [all] the strategies and the deceits of the devil." (v. 11)

Strategies means act of devising or careful plans. *Deceits* means an attempt to trick or cause to accept as true what is false.

Here, God explains how to fight in this battle. It is *NOT* coming against our fears, attacks of panic and anxiety in our own strength, trying to muster up confidence, or using the things the world has to offer—which only leads to more enslavement and bondage to them.

Psalm 33:16 states, "No king is saved by the great size and power of his army; a mighty man is not delivered by [his] much strength."

Psalm 108:11–13 states, "Have you not cast us off, O God? And will you not go forth, O God, with our armies?" (v. 11)

"Give us help against the adversary, for vain is the help of man." (v. 12)

"Through and with God, we shall do valiantly, for he it is who shall tread down our adversaries." (v. 13)

The word *valiantly*, according to *Webster*, means strength of mind or spirit that enables a man to encounter danger with firmness or personal bravery.

Wow! What a revelation here God is showing us—that if we go through and face our attacks with God and standing on his Word, he will give us the ability to persevere with firmness and personal bravery.

God directs us in the book of Ephesians to put on this whole armor that *HE* supplies in his Word. Then, he says, we will be successful in standing up to the careful planning of the tricks of the devil. The Word is the last place the devil wants you to go for help because he knows there and only there is where he is defeated. Then, he has to go and crawl back into his hole, so to speak, until he devises something else to attack you with, just hoping you'll take the bait.

GOD PROMISES

Deuteronomy 28:7 states, "The Lord shall cause your enemies who rise up against you to be defeated before your face; they shall come out against you one way and flee before you seven ways."

James 4:7 states, "So be subject [web: owing obedience or allegiance to the power of another] to God. Resist [web: exert one's self as to counteract] the devil [stand firm against him], and he will flee from you."

So, how do we resist the devil? By flooding our hearts and minds with the Word of God and being obedient to him because this is our weapon against the evil one! Let's continue in Ephesians.

Ephesians 6:12 states, "For we are not wrestling with flesh and blood but against the despotisms [web: a ruler exercising power abusively or oppressively] against the powers, against [the master spirits who are the] world rulers of this present darkness, against the spirit forces of wickedness in the heavenly [supernatural] sphere."

We are not fighting within our flesh or other people. God directly tells us whom we are wrestling with. He wants us to know who our enemy is, and many people are not aware of this fact and instead, put blame or guilt on themselves or others, which is another deceitful thought Satan loves for us to dwell on. Remember, he (Satan) is a liar!

GOD INSTRUCTS US TO USE OUR WEAPONS

Ephesians 6:13–16 states, "Therefore, put on Gods complete armor that you may be able to resist and stand [web: to tolerate without flinching or bear courageously] your ground on the evil day [of danger] and having done all [the crisis demands] to stand firmly in your place." (v. 13)

"Stand [tolerate without flinching, bear courageously] therefore [hold your ground], having tightened the belt of truth around your loins and having put on the breastplate [armor for the breast] of integrity [web: firm adherence to a code, God's Word] and of moral rectitude [web: the quality or state of being correct in judgment or procedure) and right standing with God." (v. 14)

"And having shod [web: furnished or equipped with a shoe] your feet in preparation [to face the enemy with the firm footed stability, the promptness and the readiness produced by the good news] of the gospel of peace." (v. 15)

The gospel of peace is the Word of God.

"Lift up over all, the covering shield of saving faith, upon which you can quench [extinguish] all the flaming missiles of the wicked [one]." (v. 16)

Here, God says to "lift up over all" the covering shield of saving faith. Faith always saves from destruction.

You may say, "Well, I don't have that much faith" or "I don't have faith like other people." Know, believer, this is another lie coming from the devil himself! God is the one who gives us faith, not something you are born with.

Romans 12:3 states, "For I say through the grace given unto me, to every man that is among you, not to think of himself more highly than he ought to think, but to think soberly, according as God hath dealt to every man the measure of faith." (KJV)

So then, how does God give us this measure of faith? We find the answer in the book of Romans.

Romans 10:17 states, "So then faith cometh by hearing and hearing by the Word of God." (KJV)

God's Word is very powerful! The more you read and study God's Word, the more your faith will increase. It is supernatural, something that cannot be explained or understood by the human mind. Of course, we have to walk out in that faith which we will get into more later in this study. So God says, if we use our shield of saving faith, we will be able to extinguish (all) the attacks of the wicked one. Let's go back to Ephesians.

Ephesians 6:17 and 18 states, "And take the helmet of salvation and the sword that the spirit wields [produces or creates] which is the Word of God." (v. 17)

"Pray at all times [on every occasion, in every season] in the spirit with all [manner of] prayer and entreaty [web: to plead with especially in order to persuade]. To that end, keep alert and watch with strong purpose and perseverance, interceding in behalf of all the saints [God's consecrated people]." (v. 18)

God instructs us here to pray continually over everything. Remember, prayer releases God's power, and our weapon against the evil one is the Word of the Living God!

Chapter
5

You Are not Alone

FIERY TRIALS

You are not alone in going through these fiery trials of fear, anxiety, and panic. There is not something mentally wrong with you or something you inherited or passed down from generation to generation, although Satan would love for you to believe that. Remember, he is a liar!

Even in present day, there are millions of people suffering from these same attacks or torments worldwide. Billions of dollars are being spent on medications, counseling and hospitals to treat these symptoms. Although, this is nothing new despite the growing chaos in the world we live in.

Many of our great leaders in God's Word who God wrought many mighty works through, suffered these same attacks. Let's look at one of the great men of God, David.

DAVID'S PRAYER WHILE UNDER ATTACK

Psalm 143:1–8 states, "Hear my prayer, O Lord, give ear to my supplications [web: a humble request] in your faithfulness answer me and in your righteousness." (v. 1)

"And enter not into judgment with your servant for in your sight no man living is [in himself] righteous or justified." (v. 2)

"For the enemy [Satan] has pursued and persecuted [web: harass, afflict, to make one suffer because of their beliefs with annoying persistent attacks] my soul [web: a person's total self], he has crushed my life down to the ground; he has made me to dwell in dark places as those who have been long dead." (v. 3)

How can we relate here to David when the enemy attacks us? Feeling our lives to have been crushed down to the ground, helpless, and in desperate need.

"Therefore is my spirit overwhelmed and faints within me [wrapped in gloom], my heart within my bosom grows numb." (v. 4)

David too felt frozen in his steps. Sounds familiar?

"I remember the days of old; I meditate on all your doings. I ponder [web: mentally think about deeply] the work of your hands." (v. 5)

During David's attacks, he began to think in depth about all the things God has done in the past, dwelling on God's Word and the things God had done for him and others in previous times.

"I spread forth my hands to you; my soul thirsts after you like a thirsty land [for water]. Selah [pause and calmly think of that]!" (v. 6)

David seeks God out as his vital necessity.—another important key to freedom is seeking God as our vital necessity.

"Answer me speedily, Oh Lord, for my spirit fails. Hide not your face from me, lest I become like those who go down into the pit [the grave]." (v. 7)

Here, David pleads with God to come quickly, or he says he could die because he admits that within himself, he is not strong enough to overcome these attacks. How desperate he must have felt, and don't we too feel that same desperation when the enemy attacks us?

"Cause me to hear your loving kindness in the morning, for on you do I lean and in you do I trust. Cause me to know the way wherein I should walk, for I lift up my inner self to you." (v. 8)

There are four very important keys in this verse David speaks of in the midst of his attacks.

1. First thing he mentions here is to cause him to hear God's loving kindness in the morning. We do this by praying, seeking, and studying God's Word first thing in the morning. It's important to note here how David mentions "in the morning." God always wants us to seek him first before we start our day. Have you ever felt all these negative thoughts attack your mind before your feet even hit the floor after awakening first thing in the morning? Right then and there is where you need to replace that first onset of attacks or negative thoughts with thoughts of the Word. Satan knows if he can get you to dwell on those lies and negative thoughts first thing in the morning, he can stress you out and mess with your emotions; and it will be harder for you to focus on God, therefore making it easier for him to mess with your day. Thus, the very first thing we need to do is always seek God first before beginning your day. There is nothing more important than spending quality time with our Lord!

2. Second thing David mentions here is he leans (web: to casts ones weight or rely on for support) on God. Many of us are taught at a very young age that in order to be successful, it is out of our own strength, but God says the opposite is true. He wants us to lean on him and only him for success. We cannot fight spiritual battles and win in our own flesh, but only God can fight our battles. And he will deliver every time.

Psalm 34:17 states, "When the righteous cry for help, the Lord hears and delivers them out of ALL their distresses and troubles."

3. Third thing David says is in you do I trust (web: to place confidence in and to depend on another, in this case God). You need to start trusting God by putting your confidence in him and not in yourself. Let's look at some examples of trust.

Psalm 22:4 and5 states, "Our fathers trusted in you; they trusted [leaned on, relied on you, and were confident] and you delivered them." (v. 4)

"They cried to you and were delivered; they trusted in, leaned on and confidently relied on you and were not ashamed or confounded or disappointed." (v. 5)

God says and does deliver us from our enemy when we put our trust in him, for he knows our enemy is too strong for us but not for our God.

Psalm 18:17 states, "He delivered me from my strong enemy and from those who hated me and abhorred [web: regard with extreme, strong dislike] me, for they were too strong for me."

4. The forth key is where David asks God, saying "cause me to know the way wherein I should walk." He asks God for instruction or wisdom as he lifts himself up to the Lord. He asks God to lead or show him the way in which to go to keep on moving and not letting the

enemy keep him frozen in his steps. How many times have we also felt like this as well? Well, start saying, "I don't know what to do, but my eyes are upon you to lead and to guide me as you promise to do so in your Word."

Psalm 18:18 and 19 states, "They confronted and came upon me in the day of my calamity, but the Lord was my stay and support." (v. 18)

"He brought me forth also into a large place; he was delivering me because he was pleased with me and delighted in me." (v. 19)

Well, the devil is perhaps trying to tell you right now that God is not pleased with you or that he does not delight in you, so this will hinder your deliverance. Not true! Another lie coming straight from the pit of hell. Let's look at the book of John where the people came to Jesus, asking him what God requires of them.

John 6:28 and 29 states, "Then they said, 'What are we to do, that we may [habitually] be working the works of God? [What are we to do to carry out what God requires?]'" (v. 28)

"Jesus replied, 'This is the work [service] that God asks of you; that you believe in the one whom he has sent [that you cleave to, trust, rely on and have faith in his messenger, Jesus]." (v. 29)

What are the things that God delights in? Let's look at the book of Jeremiah.

Jeremiah 9:24 states, "But let him who glories, glory in this: that he understands and knows me [personally and practically, directly discerning and recognizing my character] that I am the Lord, who practices loving kindness, judgment and righteousness in the earth for in these things I delight says the Lord."

God delights in those of us who know him personally and know that his qualities are that of love, kindness, judgment and righteousness. Let's continue, in the book of Psalm 143, to David's prayer.

Psalm 143:9–12 states, "Deliver me, Oh Lord, from my enemies [Satan and his helpers); I flee to you to hide [web: to conceal for shelter or protection] me." (v. 9)

"Teach [web: provide instruction] me to do your will, for you are my God. Let your good spirit lead me into a level [web: steady, unwavering, calm] country and into the land of uprightness." (v. 10)

"Save my life, O Lord, for your names sake, in your righteousness, bring my life out of trouble and free me from distress [web: anguish of body or mind]." (v. 11)

"And in your mercy and loving kindness, cut off my enemies and destroy all those who afflict [web: to distress so severely as to cause persistent suffering or anguish] my inner self, for I am your servant." (v. 12)

Note here where David says, "Who afflict my inner self." This is what the enemy or Satan tries to do, to cause fear and afflict our inner selves.

These verses of scripture were eye opening for me. God had shown me that there wasn't something wrong with me and that these attacks on one's self had been going on way back in biblical times to some of the greatest men and women of God; but through these great fiery trials, many miracles and acts of God were performed. There's an old saying, "Greater the purpose, greater the trial." Do not be deceived, believer. Believe the truth of God's Word!

This is just one example here in the Bible, where we see these attacks trying to defeat one of Gods people. Many of God's people expressing fear are recorded throughout the Bible, but God always says to "FEAR NOT"!

SECRET TO VICTORIOUS LIVING

There is a secret to victorious living that Paul speaks of in the book of Philippians.

Philippians 4:12 and 13 states, "I know how to be abased [web: lower physically] and live humbly [web: spirit of submission] in straightened [web: situation of perplexity or distress] circumstances, and I know how to enjoy plenty and live in abundance. I have learned in any and all circumstances the secret of facing any situation, whether well fed or going hungry, having a sufficiency and enough to spare or going without and being in want." (v. 12)

"I have strength [web: the power of resisting attack] for all things in Christ who empowers [web: make one able to do something, enable] me. [I am ready for anything and am equal to anything through him who infuses inner strength into me; I am self-sufficient in Christ's sufficiency]." (v. 13)

Here, through Paul and his life's experiences, God gives us the "secret" of facing any situation, which is through Christ. He is the one who gives us the power and ability to be victorious over attacks and that not of ourselves. Have faith in Christ!

HOW DO WE HAVE FAITH IN CHRIST?

Colossians 1:4a states, "For I have heard of your faith in Christ [amplified: the leaning of your entire human personality on him in absolute trust and confidence in his power, wisdom, and goodness)."

God wants us to lean our whole being on him and not on ourselves (our frail human flesh). We don't have the power to fight these spiritual battles within our flesh but must lean on our Lord and King, and then, he promises, he will defeat our enemy.

2 Corinthians 4:7–8 states, "However we possess this precious treasure [the divine light of the Gospel] in [frail, human] vessels of earth, that the grandeur and exceeding greatness of the power may be shown to be from God and not from ourselves." (v. 7)

"We are hedged in [pressed] on every side [troubled and oppressed in every way] but not cramped or crushed; we suffer embarrassments and are perplexed [web: filled with uncertainty, full of difficulty] and unable to find a way out but not driven to despair." (v. 8)

Don't be surprised when your trials or difficulties arise. God is fully aware of these things as he tells us here in this verse. He wants us to seek him out and obtain the wisdom he sets forth in his Word by praying and asking so that we can obtain that truth which will set us free.

James 1:5 states, "If any of you is deficient in wisdom, let him ask of the giving God [who gives] to everyone liberally and ungrudgingly, without reproaching or faultfinding, and it will be given him."

Matthew 7:8 states, "For everyone who keeps on asking receives and he who keeps on seeking finds; and to him who keeps on knocking, [the door] will be opened."

2 Corinthians 4:9 states, "We are pursued [persecuted and hard driven], but not deserted to stand alone: we are struck down to the ground, but never struck out and destroyed."

God never promises that we won't suffer while we are in this world. In fact, Jesus forewarns us that we will suffer trials.

John 16:33 states, "I have told you these things, so that in me, you may have [perfect] peace and confidence. In the world you will have tribulation and trials and distress and frustration; but be of good cheer [take courage; be confident, certain, undaunted]! For I have overcome the world. [I have deprived it of power to harm you and have conquered it for you]."

Wow! What a revelation Jesus gives us here!

When God first started opening up these truths to me, I started to feel somewhat afraid of the devil and his power. I would think, "If he has the power to attack me physically this strongly, what else can he do to me?" Of course, God showed me that this was just another thought Satan was trying to present to my mind, using intimidation and perhaps yours as well. But thanks be to our Lord, Master, and King, that he is always a step ahead and even addressed this too in his Word. To him

(God) lies all truth and wisdom. He gave me this truth as found in the following passage.

Luke 10:19 and 20 states, "Behold! I have given you authority and power to trample upon serpents and scorpions and [physical and mental strength and ability] over all the power that the enemy [possesses] and nothing shall in any way harm you." (v. 19)

"Nevertheless, do not rejoice at this, that the spirits are subject to you but rejoice that your names are enrolled in heaven." (v. 20)

Remember, Satan brings suffering, but God brings deliverance through his power to those of us who put our trust and reliance on him.

Psalm 34:19 states, "Many evils [web: causing discomfort; forces repelling one another; something that brings sorrow, distress, or calamity] confront the [consistently] righteous, but the Lord delivers [web: sets free, brings liberation, or rescues] him out of them all!"

God promises to set us free from all attacks!

Chapter
6

Winning the Battle

FEAR VERSUS FAITH

God gives instruction to us, all through his Word, to have FAITH! Satan always tries to intimidate us through fear, while God gives freedom through faith. Remember, we are all in a spiritual battle, one that can only be won through and with God. As I stated previously, there are spiritual weapons for this warfare. Satan's greatest weapon is fear while God's greatest weapon is faith. Remember what God tells us in the book of Ephesians.

Ephesians 6:16 states, "Lift up overall the [covering] shield of saving faith, upon which you can quench all the flaming missiles of the wicked [one]."

Here, God denotes that our enemy, Satan, will attack us (flaming missiles of the wicked), but faith will cause his attacks to cease through our faith in God and his promises to deliver.

WHAT IS FAITH?

God explains what faith is in the book of Hebrews.

Hebrews 11:1 states, "Now faith is the assurance [the confirmation, the title deed] of the things [we] hope for, being proof of things [we] do not see and the conviction of their reality [faith perceiving, as a real fact, what is not revealed to the senses)."

Webster defines faith as a firm belief in something for which there is no proof. In other words, faith is believing in something that you can't see by your five senses. Yet God says to have this faith. Faith in what? In him and his promises in his Word.

God is not pleased when he sees us his children being defeated by fear. He loves us and wants to see us walking in absolute trust and confidence in him—always with the assurance that he will help, deliver, and restore all the enemy is trying to take away or has taken away already. Therefore, God is not pleased when he sees us, his children, not walking by this faith that he instructs.

Hebrews 11:6 states, "But without faith, it is impossible to please and be satisfactory to him. For whoever would come near to God must [necessarily] believe that God exists and that he is a rewarder [web: a recompense, a return for something suffered] of those who earnestly [web: proceeding from an intense and serious state of mind] and diligently [web: steady, earnest and energetic application and effort; painstakingly] seek him [out]."

God wants us to have an undying need for him as a land that has no water.

Psalm 63:1 states, "O God, You are my God, earnestly will I seek you; my inner self thirsts for you, my flesh longs and is faint for you in a dry and weary land where no water is."

Psalm 63:8 states, "My whole being follows hard after you and clings closely to you; your right hand upholds me."

God wants us to stick or remain close to him always, never going astray. Have you ever noticed when you stray from God, things begin to unravel and become out of balance? When you don't pray and continue in his Word, giving him thanks and praise, you are straying from God. God says to continue in his Word. This is what Jesus did night and day, and God instructs us to do the same.

John 8:31 and 32 states, "Then said Jesus to those Jews which believed on him, if ye continue [web: to maintain without interruption a course or action] in my Word, then are ye my disciples indeed." (KJV)

"And ye shall know [web: have experience of, be convinced or certain of exclusive knowledge or information] the truth and the truth shall make you free." (v. 32)

Here, Jesus gives a promise for freedom is to continue in his Word. It doesn't mean reading or praying five minutes here and ten minutes there, although, of course, there is little profit to doing this but not if you want to live a life with the freedom that our Lord intended for you to live. You will find that, as you begin to really seek God out and begin a real application and determination to study his Word, that will be the sweetest and most valuable time spent above anyone else here on this earth, and the things of this earth will grow strangely dim. In other words, the cares, anxieties, and things pertaining to this world will not be as important or prominent to you. But your eyes will be turned to the heavenly kingdom and the world in which to come.

FAITH ACCOMPLISHES

Hebrews 11:2 states, "For by it [faith, trust, and holy favor, born of faith) the men of old had divine testimony borne to them and obtained a good report."

Our God never disappoints those who put their trust in him!

Hebrews 10:23 states, "So let us seize [web: to understand fully and distinctly] and hold fast and retain [web: keep in mind or memory] without wavering [web: fluctuate in opinion, allegiance, or direction] the hope we cherish and confess our acknowledgement of it, for he who promised is reliable [web: dependable, giving the same result on successive trials, sure] and faithful to his Word."

Hebrews 10:35 states, "Do not therefore fling away your fearless confidence, for it carries a great and glorious compensation [web: a psychological mechanism by which feelings of inferiority, frustration, or failure in one field are counterbalanced by achievement in another] of reward."

In other words, God says to not let the fear in which the enemy presents intimidate you or cause you to lose your confidence in him (God), and he will turn your frustrations into achievements by and through him. Therefore, we must walk in this faith if we want to be pleasing to God. Let's look at it in a mathematical sense. God is pleased when we are full of joy and confidence. He gives us a formula, so to speak, to achieve this joy:

JUST LIKE 1+1=2>>>>>>>>>FEAR + FAITH = JOY AND
                                                                         SUCCESS

                                      ^   ^   ^

                                      ^   ^   ^

                          (attacks of the   (Gods   (Freedom &
                           enemy)   instruction-   Liberation)
                                              Our weapon)

Start saying this every day, over and over: I will not fear; I will walk by faith!

WALK BY FAITH

2 Corinthians 5:7 states, "For we walk by faith not by sight or appearance."

No matter how bad things may appear or how panicked, fearful, or anxious you may be feeling, still move forward in the face of fear, walking in faith, trusting God to see you through. He will bring you out victoriously as he promises to do so in his Word.

God never brings more on us than we can handle and loves it when we totally lean and rely on him for all things that trouble us.

1 Corinthians 10:13 states, "There hath no temptation taken you but such as is common to man, but God is faithful, who will not suffer you to be tempted above that ye are able but will with the temptation also make a way to escape that ye may be able to bear it." (KJV)

Webster defines *bear* as "to move while being held up and supported, to put up with something trying or painful." God says he is faithful to his Word and can be trusted if we do those things he instructs, which is to lean on him, trusting him in any and all things. We need to quit listening to the lies of the devil and trust God!

By faith, God wrought many mighty works despite the opposition and circumstances.

Hebrews 11:4 and 5 states, "[Prompted, actuated] By faith, Abel brought God a better and more acceptable sacrifice than Cain because of which it was testified of him, that he was righteous [that he was upright and in right standing with God], and God bore witness by accepting and acknowledging his gifts. And though he died, yet [through the incident] he is still speaking." (v. 4)

"Because of faith, Enoch was caught up and transferred to heaven so that he did not have a glimpse of death, and he was not found because God had translated him. For even before he was taken to heaven, he received testimony [still on record] that he had pleased and been satisfactory to God." (v. 5)

Hebrews 11:7–12 states, "[Prompted] By faith, Noah being forewarned by God concerning events of which as yet, there was no visible sign, took heed and diligently and reverently constructed and prepared an ark for the deliverance of his own family. By this [his faith which relied on God], he passed judgment and sentence on the world's unbelief and became an heir and possessor of righteousness [that relation of being right into which God puts the person who has faith]." (v. 7)

"[Urged on] By faith, Abraham, when he was called, obeyed and went forth to a place which he was destined to receive as an inheritance, and he went, although he did not know or trouble his mind about where he was to go." (v. 8)

"[Prompted by faith] He dwelt as a temporary resident in the land which was designated in the promise [of God, though he was a stranger] in a strange country, living in tents with Isaac and Jacob." (v. 9)

"For he was [waiting expectantly and confidently] looking forward to the city which has fixed and firm foundations, whose architect and builder is God." (v. 10)

"Because of faith, Sara herself also received physical power to conceive a child, even when she was long past the age for it, because she considered [God] who has given her the promise to be reliable and trustworthy and true to his Word." (v. 11)

"So from one man, though he was physically as good as dead, there have sprung descendants whose number is as the stars of heaven and as countless as the innumerable sands on the seashore." (v. 12)

So we see from all these, believers, that they did not look at circumstances or what they could conceive in their own limited human minds but trusted God and believed and relied on him to bring what he had promised. They, therefore, saw the wonderful miracles that God wrought through them.

Don't you want to experience what these believers experienced in their lives too? Then, you too must live your life based on the promises of the Word and not lean on your own understanding, knowing that our God is a faithful God and what he has promised, he is also able to perform and *CAN* be trusted.

Let's look at a few more examples God shows in his Word of walking in this faith.

MOSES WALKED BY FAITH

When God called on Moses to free the people of Israel from slavery, the Egyptians were chasing them to kill them when they tried to flee Egypt. The people were naturally afraid and were running for their lives when Moses told them to put their trust in God. They now came upon the sea and there was no place to go.

Exodus 14:13–15 states, "Moses told the people, 'Fear not; stand still [firm, confident, undismayed] and see the salvation of the Lord which he will work for you today. For the Egyptians you have seen today you shall never see again.'" (v. 13)

"The Lord will fight for you, and you shall hold your peace and remain at rest." (v. 14)

This is what God wants us to do in the midst of our battles—to know the Lord will fight for us, and he will give us peace and rest.

"The Lord said to Moses, 'Why do you cry to me? Tell the people of Israel to go forward!'" (v. 15)

Important to note here that even though Moses was telling the people to trust in God, he was still crying out to God for help. I'm sure even he was struggling with fear during this battle. After all, we are all human, and our God understands that. But what did God tell him to do? He told him to tell the people to "GO FORWARD".

God is instructing us to do the same, and that is to Go Forward in the face of fear. This is a very important key and revelation from God he is giving us through his Word. When the enemy attacks us, we are instructed to move forward in the face of fear during the enemies attacks—not when things have subsided or when we're feeling better but in the midst of the attack. This is where God will bring the victory! Let's see what happened now as the people did as the Lord instructed.

Exodus 14:21 and 22 states, "Then Moses stretched out his hand over the sea and the Lord caused the sea to go back by a strong east wind all that night and made the sea dry land and the waters were divided." (v. 21)

"And the Israelites went into the midst of the sea on dry ground, the waters being a wall to them on their right hand and on their left." (v. 22)

Picture this scene in your mind. Our God not only says he will deliver us from trouble, but he is also able and can, in a most miraculous way inconceivable to our human minds. God can do anything, and his resources are limitless! Why wouldn't you want to put your trust in a limitless God who promises to help you in your attacks? Don't let the enemy stop you with his lies but trust God and Go Forward! *DO NOT LET FEAR STOP YOU*

The Egyptians continued in their pursuit after the Israelites while the Israelites ran for their lives, chasing them in the midst of the sea. Then, God made a pillar of fire to stop their pursuit.

Exodus 14:24 states, "And in the morning watch, the Lord, through a pillar of fire and cloud looked down on the host of the Egyptians and discomfited [web: frustrated the plans of, put into a state of perplexity and embarrassment] them."

This is what God will do for us when the enemy attacks us when we walk out in this faith. He will frustrate our enemy's (Satan's) plans to hurt us, and he will be perplexed and embarrassed! This is God's Word, believer, and he had this written for our learning so that when we are faced with battles, we would in turn heed his Word and believe, walking out in this faith as Moses did.

Exodus 14:25–28 states, "And bound [clogged, took off] their chariot wheels, making them drive heavily; and the Egyptians said, Let us flee from the face of Israel; for the Lord fights for them against the Egyptians! (v. 25)

"Then the Lord said to Moses, Stretch out your hand over the sea, that the waters may come again upon the Egyptians, upon their chariots and horsemen." (v. 26)

"So Moses stretched forth his hand over the sea, and the sea returned to its strength and normal flow when the morning appeared; and the Egyptians fled into it [being met by it], and the Lord overthrew the Egyptians and shook them off into the midst of the sea." (v. 27)

"The waters returned and covered the chariots, the horsemen, and all the host of Pharaoh that pursued them; not even one of them remained." (v. 28)

The Israelites were delivered from the enemy by the great and all powerful hand of God because of one man, Moses, who made the decision to walk by faith in his God and directed the Israelites to do the same.

JONAH, BY FAITH, WAS SET FREE

Even Jonah saw the mighty hand of God in his life. In the book of Jonah, God saw wickedness in the city of Nineveh. He told Jonah to go and tell the people of Nineveh that he (God) did not like what the people were doing and wanted them to repent and change their ways. But Jonah did not obey the Lord and tried to flee by ship to another city called Tarshish and ended up getting swallowed up by a whale. Let's read the account.

Jonah 1:1–5 states, "Now the word of the Lord came to Jonah, son of Amittai, saying;" (v. 1)

"Arise, go to Nineveh, that great city, and proclaim against it, for their wickedness has come up before me." (v. 2)

"But Jonah rose up to flee to Tarshish from being in the presence of the Lord [as his prophet] and went down to Joppa and found a ship going to Tarshish [the most remote of the Phoenician trading places known then]. So he paid the appointed fare and went down into the ship to go with them to Tarshish from being in the presence of the Lord [as his servant and minister]." (v. 3)

"But the Lord sent out a great wind upon the sea, and there was a violent tempest on the sea so that the ship was about to be broken." (v. 4)

"Then the mariners were afraid, and each man cried to his god; and they cast the goods that were in the ship into the sea to lighten it for them. But Jonah had gone down into the inner part of the ship and had laid down and was fast asleep." (v. 5)

"So the captain came and said to him, 'What do you mean, you sleeper? Arise, call upon your God! Perhaps your God will give a thought to us so that we may not perish.'" (v. 6)

When you are faced with a battle and are under attack, the first thing you need to do is call upon God and pray he will guide you in his wisdom to let you know what to do.

Then the people on the ship ended up casting lots to see on whose account this evil befell them, and the lot fell on Jonah. Jonah explained to them what he had done, fleeing from the Lord's presence. Let's continue now.

Jonah 1:11 and 12 states, "Then they said to him, 'What shall we do to you, that the sea may subside and be calm for us? For the sea became more and more [violently] tempestuous." (v. 11)

"And he [Jonah] said to them, 'Take me up and cast me into the sea; so shall the sea become calm for you, for I know that it is because of me that this great tempest has come upon you.'" (v. 12)

Jonah 1:15–17 states, "So they took up Jonah and cast him into the sea, and the sea ceased from its raging." (v. 15)

"Then the men [reverently and worshipfully] feared the Lord exceedingly, and they offered a sacrifice to the Lord and made vows." (v. 16)

God used this incident and made believers out of these men! God can use the bad things that happen to us in our lives for his good as well.

"Now the Lord had prepared and appointed a great fish to swallow up Jonah. And Jonah was in the belly of the fish three days and three nights." (v. 17)

How fearful Jonah must have been. Can you imagine this—being in the belly of a fish, even for a second—never mind three days and three nights? But what did Jonah do? Out of his desperate need, *he prayed to the Lord!* Let's continue now to chapter 2.

Jonah 2:1 and 2 states, "Then Jonah prayed to the Lord his God from the fish's belly." (v. 1)

"And said, 'I cried out of my distress to the Lord, and he heard me; out of the belly of Sheol cried I, and you heard my voice.'" (v. 2)

Whenever we cry out to the Lord, he hears our voice. Prayer is using your faith.

God not only heard Jonah's voice when he prayed in faith to the Lord, but he also delivered him as we see in the later part of this chapter.

Jonah 2:10 states, "And the Lord spoke to the fish, and it vomited out Jonah upon the dry land."

Amazing, isn't it! God spoke to the fish, and even the fish obeyed! God is in control of everything and is all powerful. All he wants from us is to believe and have faith in him in any and all circumstances, no matter how grim or impossible it may seem.

After all that happened to Jonah, he did indeed obey God and went and spoke to the people of Nineveh.

As God was opening up these truths to me, I thought, what a great God we serve who has all power and might to help us overcome anything in this world. No matter how much the enemy presses upon us, he promises to deliver every time. He is certainly greatly to be praised and worshipped!

DAVID CHOSE TO WALK BY FAITH

Let's look at another story of faith where David, just a youth, defeated the giant Philistine by faith and with a little sling shot, while the whole army fled in fear.

1 Samuel 17:1–4 states, "Now the Philistines gathered together their armies for battle and were assembled at Socoh, which belongs to Judah, and encamped between Socoh and Azekah in Ephes-dammim." (v. 1)

"Saul and the men of Israel were encamped in the Valley of Elah and drew up in battle array against the Philistines." (v. 2)

"And the Philistines stood on a mountain on one side and Israel stood on a mountain on the other side, with the valley between them." (v. 3)

"And a champion went out of the camp of the Philistines named Goliath of Gath, whose height was six cubits and a span [almost ten feet]." (v. 4)

This giant was heavily armored, powerful, and very intimidating to the armies of Israel.

Let's continue in 1 Samuel 17:8–14. "Goliath stood and shouted to the ranks of Israel, 'Why have you come out to draw up for battle? Am I not a Philistine, and are you not servants of Saul? Choose a man for yourselves and let him come down to me.'" (v. 8)

"If he is able to fight with me and kill me, then we will be your servants; but if I prevail against him and kill him, then you shall be our servants and serve us." (v. 9)

"And the Philistine said, 'I defy the ranks of Israel this day; give me a man, that we may fight together.'" (v. 10)

"When Saul and all Israel heard those words of the Philistine, they were dismayed and greatly afraid." (v. 11)

Right here at the onset of the attack of the enemy is where the armies of Israel had to make a choice, whether to back down in fear or move forward as God instructs us all to do.

"David was the son of an Ephrathite of Bethlehem in Judah named Jesse, who had eight sons. [Jesse] in the days of Saul was old, advanced in years." (v. 12)

"[His] three eldest sons had followed Saul into battle. Their names were Eliab, the first born; next, Abinadab; and third, Shammah." (v. 13)

"David was the youngest. The three eldest followed Saul." (v. 14)

David was not fighting in the battle but was taking care of his father's sheep when his father (Jesse) told him to go and take food to his brothers and to the commander of the camp of the army of Israel. The armies were in full battle between Israel and the Philistines when David arrived to where his brothers were.

1 Samuel 17: 23–26 states, "As they talked, behold, Goliath, the champion, the Philistine of Gath, came forth from the Philistine ranks and spoke the same words as before, and David heard him." (v. 23)

"And all the men of Israel, when they saw the man, fled from him, terrified." (v. 24)

"And the Israelites said, 'Have you seen this man who has come out? Surely he has come out to defy Israel; and the man who kills him, the king will enrich with great riches and will give him his daughter and make his father's house free [from taxes and service] in Israel.'" (v. 25)

"And David said to the men standing by him, 'What shall be done for the man who kills this Philistine and takes away the reproach from Israel? For who is this uncircumcised Philistine that he should defy the armies of the living God?'" (v. 26)

Remember, Israel is a chosen Holy Land by God himself, and those who fight for Israel will be blessed and those who rise up against it will be destroyed.

David was not intimidated by this giant, Goliath, and went to King Saul and spoke to him.

I Samuel 17:32 and 33 states, "David said to Saul, Let no man's heart fail because of this Philistine; your servant will go out and fight with him." (v. 32)

"And Saul said to David, You are not able to go to fight against this Philistine. You are only an adolescent, and he has been a warrior from his youth." (v. 33)

Then David began to tell Saul how he tended to his father's sheep and when a lion or bear came, he killed it because the Lord had delivered him. The story now continues.

I Samuel 17:37 states, "David said, 'The Lord Who delivered me out of the paw of the lion and out of the paw of the bear, he will deliver me out of the hand of this Philistine.' And Saul said to David, 'Go and the Lord be with you!'" (v. 37)

David made the choice to walk by faith in God rather than look at the circumstances.

God is trying to show us something here in this record that no matter how big the giants present themselves to us, he wants us to continue to walk by faith—faith in him, that he will deliver us. What are the giants in your life that are troubling you? Is fear and intimidation of the enemy trying to keep you immobilized or to run or flee in terror? Well, this is when you need to take that step of faith, stand your ground, and see the deliverance of the Lord.

I Samuel 17:40–50 states, "Then he [David] took his staff in his hand and chose five smooth stones out of the brook and put them in his shepherd's [lunch] bag [a whole kid's skin slung from his shoulder] in his pouch, and his sling was in his hand, and he drew near the Philistine." (v. 40)

"The Philistine came on and drew near to David, the man who bore the shield going before him." (v. 41)

"And when the Philistine looked around and saw David, he scorned and despised him, for he was but an adolescent, with a healthy reddish color and a fair face." (v. 42)

"And the Philistine said to David, 'Am I a dog, that you should come to me with sticks?' And the Philistine cursed David by his gods." (v. 43)

The enemy was trying to intimidate David by having him look by his five senses rather than trusting God by saying, Really! You come to me with sticks and plan to defeat me.

Picture this story, believer. All the armies backed down to this giant Philistine, Goliath, but here, David, a youth had more faith than all of them and was willing to go forward, relying on God to take this giant down and deliver the people of Israel. What faith David had! Remember, faith is believing in something you can't see by your five senses, believing in something to take place that hasn't happened yet.

"The Philistine said to David, 'Come to me and I will give your flesh to the birds of the air and the beasts of the field.'" (v. 44)

Still, the enemy was trying to intimidate David and shake his faith.

"Then said David to the Philistine, 'You come to me with a sword, a spear, and a javelin, but I come to you in the name of the Lord of hosts, the God of the ranks of Israel, whom you have defied.'" (v. 45)

David told the giant that he comes to him with all this armor and power, but all David needed to do was come to him in the name of the Lord who has more power than him. What faith David had!

"This day the Lord will deliver you into my hand and I will smite you and cut off your head. And I will give the corpses of the army of the Philistines this day to the birds of the air and the wild beasts of the earth, that all the earth may know that there is a God in Israel." (v. 46)

Wow! Where did this boldness come from? When you stand for God, he fills you with boldness and confidence in him! But it comes when you take that step of faith, not before. Many of us want that confidence before and therefore, do not step out in the midst of our battles. But God says, "Move forward in the face of fear!" Now, here comes the most important key to remember: the battles we face are *NOT* our battles to fight but Gods.

"And all this assembly shall know that the Lord saves not with a sword and spear; for the battle is the Lord's and he will give you into our hands." (v. 47)

"When the Philistine came forward to meet David, David ran quickly toward the battle line to meet the Philistine." (v. 48)

David did not hesitate to stop and think about the situation but ran quickly to meet the battle head on. This is another thing we must do in order to receive deliverance. Satan would love to have us keep thinking about it over and over in our minds, but God says to run to battle and see the deliverance of the Lord.

"David put his hand into his bag and took out a stone and slung it, and it struck the Philistine sinking into his forehead and he fell on his face to the earth." (v. 49)

"So David prevailed over the Philistine with a sling and with a stone and struck down the Philistine and slew him. But no sword was in David's hand." (v. 50)

All these men that God used were people (human) as we all are, but rather than being controlled by fears, doubts, and panic, they all chose to take that step of faith in the midst of their negative circumstance. Rather than allowing the enemy to keep them frozen in their paths, they chose to trust and have confidence in God, that he would see them through and deliver them. They pushed through in faith—believing, trusting, and relying on God; and he gave them victory.

All over the Word, over and over, God emphasizes to have faith in him. Don't wonder why the attacks from hell are so strong against you, trying to shake you from your core. Satan is fully aware that if you decide, in the midst of his turmoil, to walk out in faith in God, that God will not only deliver you from his hand; but he will be defeated. He does not like defeat, and he can present things to us that seem so real but instead are nothing but lies. You need to make a decision: Are you going to believe what God says?

Remember once again, God says, above all, to take the shield of faith wherewith we can quench all the flaming missiles of the wicked one. The battle is between him and our God.

2 Chronicles 20:17 states, "You shall not need to fight in this battle, take your positions, stand still and see the deliverance of the Lord [who is] with you, O Judah and Jerusalem. Fear not nor be dismayed [web: sudden loss of courage or resolution from alarm or fear]. Tomorrow, go out against them, for the Lord is with you."

Where God says, O Judah and Jersusalem, when writing on your index card, put your name there. This is something the Lord had me do, making it personal to me.

Example: You shall not need to fight in this battle (your name here). Fear not nor be dismayed. Tomorrow, go out against them, for the Lord is with you!

What a loving and dependable God we serve.

Amen.

Chapter
7

Pressing through in Faith—Believing

BEGIN WALKING OUT IN FAITH

Now you know who is attacking you and why and have learned we are all in a spiritual battle. We need to come to God early and pray, seeking him as our vital necessity, knowing our greatest weapon for this warfare is FAITH. Now what? You may say, "Okay, Lord, I believe you love me. I believe your Word is truth… But!" There's that big word of doubt, *BUT*! Satan will always try to present to your mind with the big *but*! I know full well from my own experience that when I was being severely attacked with total fear, anxiety, and panic, I told the Lord, "But my whole body is trembling and is full of anxiety and fear. I've been barely sleeping, and I know you want me to have faith, but how can I do anything when all hell is coming against me and my whole body is in full distress? I just want to run and hide myself!"

God's answer to me was, "Do it anyway!" He led me to this verse of scripture in the book of Isaiah.

Isaiah 43:1b and 2 states, "Fear not, for I have redeemed you [ransomed you by paying a price instead of leaving you captives]: I have called you by your name; you are mine." (v. 1b)

"When you pass through the waters, I will be with you and through the rivers, they will not overwhelm you. When you walk through the fire; you will not be burned or scorched, nor will the flame kindle upon you." (v. 2)

Isaiah 43:3a states, "For I am the Lord your God, the Holy one of Israel, your Savior."

God wants us to press through despite how we feel. This was a huge revelation to me! God gives us five extremely important things here in these verses:

1. First thing he says is "Fear Not, for I have redeemed you." The word *redeemed* means to be free from what distresses. (web) God says, don't be afraid; I have freed you. Now, we have to claim that freedom.

2. Secondly, paying a price instead of leaving you captives (web: taken and held as prisoner by an enemy in war). God says he will not leave us as our enemies' prisoners but will set us free.

3. Thirdly, he called you by your name: You are mine. God actually calls us by our names and tells us we belong to him. We are his children; he knows your name.

4. Fourthly, when you pass through the waters, through rivers, through fire—which is interpreted, according to The Word Translation, as troubles of any kind— God will be with you. God wants us to move forward despite opposition and promises to be there for us and bring us out victoriously through any and all our troubles.

5. Lastly, he says, I am the Lord your God, the Holy One, Your Savior (web: one that saves from danger or destruction). God says he is our God, Holy One (web: awesome, frightening and beyond belief, filled with superhuman power).

God promises us here, that if we move forward in the face of any troubles, he will be there to help us achieve victory and not leave us captive to the enemies' attacks. Why? The answer is found in the next verse.

Isaiah 43:4a states, "Because you are precious [web: a person of superior standing] and because I love you."

This is amazing how God views us! He sees us as people of superior standing in this world. Now you know the devil does not want you to believe that! That's why we find so many people thinking themselves to be worthless because of all the thoughts that we buy in to when he presents them to our minds—thoughts of condemnation, worthlessness, evil, and the list goes on and on. Don't forget what a liar he is the next time you find your mind getting attacked by these evil and negative thoughts about yourself. Put them out of your mind at his onset and remember how God sees you and speak/confess that aloud! The word *love* here in the Hebrew is "aheb," which is always God's love toward us, his children, never our love toward God. His love is supreme, beyond human ability.

When the enemy can keep you from moving forward and intimidate you through his fear tactics, then he's got you and wins. Have you ever noticed, sometimes, when being under attack, there is no reasoning behind your fear? You just feel anxious and don't understand why. It doesn't even make sense. There's no reason to fear, yet your whole body trembles; your heart palpitates, and you just want to run. At one time, I can recall a pastor sharing how he was on an airplane and suddenly felt this attack of anxiety and panic come over him out of nowhere. The attack was so strong that he even contemplated jumping out of the airplane. Many of us who have experienced these attacks can well relate to this pastor. That is indeed an attack coming straight from the pit of hell. Satan hates us with an absolute cruel hatred and will do anything he can to distract us from serving our God in any way he can. He will do anything to try to stop us from taking that step of faith and trust in our God. That's why he presses so hard in his attacks. He is not only trying to stop you but wants to destroy you as well.

But God, on the other hand, tells us to use our weapon of faith during the battle, instructing us to move forward in confidence and trust that he will deliver us from the enemies attacks.

Deuteronomy 28:6, 7 and 10 states, "Blessed shall you be when you come in and blessed shall you be when you go out." (v. 6)

"The Lord shall cause your enemies who rise up against you to be defeated before your face, they shall come out against you one way and flee before you seven ways." (v. 7)

"And all the people of the earth shall see that you are called by the name of the Lord and they shall be afraid of you." (v. 10)

God is reassuring us here in his promise to us that when we make the decision to keep moving forward with him despite the attacks of the enemy, he will cause our enemies to be defeated before our face.

When I was first being hit with the attack of panic and anxiety, just normal everyday things seemed hard to do. I found myself in a state of dread days before I needed to do something. The enemy was trying to keep me bound up in my home. I can remember—I had an appointment to get my hair done which I've done hundreds of times in the past now—finding myself being hit with even more anxiety days before my appointment. Of course, this made me feel frustrated but kept God's Word up in my mind by reading and studying it throughout the day, constantly asking for his help. The night before, I could feel the attacks getting stronger. I could feel this anxiety attacking my mind and body and repeatedly kept giving it to God. I went to sleep at 10:00 p.m. that evening only to find myself wide awake at 11:00 p.m. I decided, after tossing and turning till around 1:30 a.m., to read and study God's Word. I was in constant prayer, trying to keep focused on the Lord and not on the attack. I finally drifted off to sleep around 4:30 a.m. only to find myself in a state of total panic once again at 6:30 a.m. I thought about cancelling my appointment but started to pray and ask God to help me get over this. He reminded me that this is an attack coming from Satan and told me to keep pressing through and go to the appointment anyway. I remember him saying, "This is not your fault. I want you to depend on my strength and not yours. I will help you and strengthen you. The battle is *NOT* yours to fight but *MINE!* Have I not told you in my Word in Numbers 23:19 that I am not a man that I should lie. I will make good on what I promised and that is to help you during your trials. Go forth trusting me, for on me, you can depend." So with my mind focused on him, seeking him as my vital necessity and on the authority of his Word, I set my face like flint in determination, got ready, and headed down to my appointment. Still, the devil was attacking my mind and body with anxiety and trembling, but I was determined to not let him stop me. Trusting God in the midst of this battle, walking out in blind faith while my whole being was in complete distress was not an easy thing to do. But I wanted to see if God could be trusted to fight this battle for me as he promised to do, so therefore, I took that step of faith despite the circumstances and chose to be obedient to what God had said. As soon as I arrived and walked through the door of the salon, *ALL ANXIETIES FLED*, and God did indeed overturn the attacks of the enemy just as he promised to do. God filled me with confidence and boldness, and his peace came over me like a rushing mighty river.

Had I chose to not take that step of faith, Satan would have won, and his plan to keep me in bondage would have succeeded; but God's desire was to set me free. What a great God we serve! He is closer than a brother and wants not only to be

Lord of our lives but our very best friend. He truly is a God of his word and *CAN BE TRUSTED*! Even though Satan had been attacking me with panic, my whole body trembling and had barely any sleep, God was there to help and come through as he promised. He will do the same for you if you put your trust in him. Press through in faith believing and let *HIM* fight the battle.

Satan knows full well that it is extremely hard to move forward when your whole being is in full distress and thus presses harder. But God gives us insight as to how to overcome his attacks, and that is to press through anyway, trusting him to deliver. And he does *DELIVER*!

TRIALS ALONG THE WAY

You have asked God to deliver you and find the opposition fighting you every step of the way. Well know, believer, Satan is not going to freely let go and let God do his work and just step aside. Remember, the battle is between him and our God, and if you stand for God, you stand in direct opposition to your enemy, the devil. There will be trials along the way—some perhaps hard to bear—but God will bring you through. Trust in him!

When Moses led the Israelites out of Egypt by the hand of God, they too experienced opposition.

Numbers 21:4 states, "And they journeyed from Mount Hor by the way to the Red Sea to go around the land of Edom and the people became impatient [depressed, much discouraged] because [of the trials] of the way."

Webster defines *trial* as a test of faith, patience, or stamina by suffering or temptation; a tryout or experiment to test quality, value, or usefulness. The next time a trial befalls you, look at it as a test of faith and tell yourself, "I am going to pass this test and trust that God will bring you out victoriously."

There has never been anyone ever recorded in the Bible that God has done his mighty works through that has not endured great trials. Why should we expect any different?

God allows trials in our lives to build our faith in him and him alone. He also uses the trials in our lives to not only help us, but to help others as well. He does not want us to depend on our own strength and ability but to always lean on him for all things. We cannot fight spiritual battles within our flesh!

It is favorable and pleasing to God if we bear patiently when suffering in trials. It builds trust in him.

1 Peter 2:19 and 20 states, "For one is regarded favorably [is approved, acceptable, and thankworthy] if, as in the sight of God, he endures the pain of unjust suffering." (v. 19)

"[After all] What kind of glory [is there in it] if, when you do wrong and are punished for it, you take it patiently? But if you bear [web: put up with something trying or painful while being held up or supported] patiently [web: bearing pains or trials calmly without complaint, steadfast despite opposition, difficulty, or adversity) with suffering [which results] when you do right and that is undeserved, it is acceptable and pleasing to God." (v. 20)

Do not misunderstand, believer. It's not that God is pleased when we suffer unjustly, but when we do bear trials without complaining, it opens up the door for God to do a mighty work; and that's where he is pleased. If we bear trials complaining and letting it overwhelm us, seeking other ways of comfort in the world rather than our God, it hinders God's complete work of deliverance, therefore making him displeased.

That's why it took the Israelites forty years to get to the promised land which in those ancient times should have only taken eleven days.

Deuteronomy 1:2 states, "It is [only] eleven days journey from Horeb by way of Mount Seir to Kadesh-barnea [on Caanan's border], yet Israel took forty years to get beyond it."

Why? The bible says they were rebellious, stiff-necked people, murmurers, and complainers.

Exodus 32:9 states, "And the Lord said to Moses, I have seen this people and behold, it is a stiff-necked people [web: haughty, proud, stubborn]."

Whenever we think our way is better or we know better than God and go outside his instruction, we become stiff-necked people. Therefore, we keep going around the same old mountains, so to speak, until we hopefully and finally surrender to his will or instruction.

Numbers 32:13a states, "And the Lord's anger was kindled against Israel and made them wander in the wilderness for forty years."

Imagine that! Taking forty years of going around and around the same mountains to get to the promised land which was only to be an eleven-day journey until the people finally surrendered to God. We need to surrender to God now and heed and follow his instruction in his Word, trusting him and being ever so thankful continually.

During the Israelites trials, even though God had been delivering them and gave them what they needed to sustain them till they reached the promised land, they still complained and even spoke against God and Moses.

Numbers 21:5 states, "And the people spoke against God and Moses. Why have you brought us out of Egypt to die in the wilderness? For there is no bread, neither is there any water and we loathe this light [contemptible, unsubstantial] manna."

They became evil in the sight of the Lord, and instead of prayer and petition and being thankful, trusting in God during their trials, they sought their own ways to deal with their circumstances. They became disobedient to God.

ENDURANCE IN HARDSHIP

God wants us to have endurance during trials.

James 1:2–4 states, "Consider it wholly joyful my brethren, whenever you are enveloped in or encounter trials of any sort or fall into various temptations." (v. 2)

Why does God say to consider it wholly joyful to encounter trials? We find the answer in the next verse.

"Be assured and understand that the trial and proving of your faith bring out endurance [web: the ability to withstand hardship, adversity, or stress] steadfastness [web: firm in belief, determination, or adherence] and patience [web: bearing pains or trials calmly without complaint]." (v. 3)

"But let endurance have full play and do a thorough work so that you may be [people] perfectly and fully developed [with no defects] lacking in nothing." (v. 4)

Trials bring about the testing of our faith. We have to ask ourselves, when the trials or attacks of the enemy comes, are we going to act out in faith, trusting God which will bring us to maturity in Christ and grow in him, bringing about freedom? Or are we going to run in fear, reaching out to the world's way of coping with the situation which only leads to more enslavement?

God's will is for us is to grow up in him; but if we choose the other route, we will keep going around the same mountains, so to speak, and be tested again and again until we choose to obey our God.

Remember, God loves you and wants to see you completely SET FREE, and the only way to achieve this freedom is by believing and obeying what he says in his Word.

Isaiah 60:1 states, "Arise from the depression and prostration [web: complete physical or mental exhaustion, powerlessness] in which circumstances have kept you-rise to a new life! Shine [be radiant with the glory of the Lord] for your light has come and the glory of the Lord has risen upon you."

God wants us to rise from our circumstances to a new life in Christ. The life he has called us to live, a life flowing in abundance. He is showing you how to live this new life by giving you insight and power through his Word. We, as believers, need to be obedient to his instruction and not for a minute let the enemy hold us back, no matter what the circumstance. To shine is to be walking by the light of the Word, trusting him (God) every step we take. Then, he says "the glory" which according to Webster: the splendor and state of utmost bliss, great gratification, or exaltation—of the Lord will rise upon you. Wow! God says if we walk by the light of the Word, the state of utmost bliss and great gratification will rise upon us! What an amazing promise!

The only way to arise from the depression and physical or mental exhaustion is to press through trials with patience in faith, believing God to bring victory every time! Remember, our enemy, the devil, wants to hold you back, but God wants to bring you through.

FEELINGS VERSUS FAITH

Feelings (Fear) > brings defeat verses
Faith (Trust) > brings victory

Do you want to walk by feelings or by faith? Only you can make the choice. Let's look at what Jesus said in the book of Matthew.

Matthew 7:13 and 14 states, "Enter through the narrow [web: tense] gate; for wide is the gate and spacious and broad is the way that leads away to destruction [web: subject to crushing defeat] and many are those who are entering through it." (v. 13)

"But the gate is narrow (Amp: contracted by pressure [web: the burden of physical or mental distress] and the way is straightened [web: coming from a trustworthy source] and compressed [web: reduced in size as by pressure] that leads away to life and few are those who find it." (v. 14)

When God had first opened up these verses of scripture to me, I was elated as he explained this to me, so that I could truly understand the meaning. I want to share this with you so that you too can grasp the true meaning of this in more clarity. Let's re-read these verses with its definitions again to unfold its true and deeper meaning:

"Enter through the tense gate, contracted by pressure of the enemy, for wide is the gate and spacious and broad is the way that leads away to crushing defeat and many are those who are entering through it." (v. 13)

"But the gate is tense, contracted by the burden of physical or mental distress [from our enemy, Satan] and the way is coming from a trustworthy source [talking about the truth of God's Word], reduced in size by pressure [attacks of the enemy] that leads away to life and few are those who find it." (v. 14)

Wow! Wow! Wow! I hope you are getting this great revelation that Jesus unfolded here!

Satan our enemy uses pressure on our physical bodies and our minds or emotions, so we won't find that life that God has called us out to live—a life filled with joy, peace, and satisfaction in him (God). Many of us give in or give heed to the things the enemy presents, and very wide is that way or gate that many people choose rather than pressing through the gate that is contracted by pressure of the enemy in faith, believing God to see us through. Satan does not want you to enter the tense gate because he knows full well that this is where you will find that true freedom.

This is why Jesus said, "Few are those who find it." "And wide is the gate that leads away to crushing defeat and many are those who are entering through it." Do you want to be one of those who is not going to be intimidated any longer by Satan's trickery?

Then you must keep pressing through in faith, believing and entering the narrow and tense gate no matter what the circumstance; and you will find God's blessings on the other side when you cross over.

The devil, our enemy, is real, people, whether you want to believe it or not. The Bible tells us so. But so is the Almighty

God whom we serve, and he is showing us answers and solutions in his Word on how to live this life. We need to use them! It's that simple. Times may be hard and, like I've said, some harder to bear; but with God, we can do the impossible.

Take that step of faith, trusting God to see you through each and every trouble or trial, and he promises to deliver each and every time. This is what he says in troubles.

Psalm 50:15 states, "And call upon me in the day of trouble; I will deliver you, and you shall honor and glorify me."

Remember: Walk by faith, not by sight, and it's when you pass through that God delivers!

1 Corinthians 10:13b states, "But God is faithful to his Word and to his compassionate [web: granted because of unusual distressing circumstances affecting an individual] nature and he [can be trusted] not to let you be tempted and tried and assayed [web: put under trial] beyond your ability and strength of resistance and power to endure but with the temptation, he will [always] provide the way out [the means of escape to a landing place] that you may be capable and strong and powerful to bear up under it patiently."

PRESS PAST HOW YOU FEEL

Do not go by your five senses (feelings or reasoning), remembering we are all in a spiritual battle, one that cannot be fought or won without our God and his instruction.

Proverbs 3:5 and 6 states, "Lean on, trust in and be confident in the Lord with all your heart and mind and do not rely on your own insight or understanding." (v. 5)

God says here "with *ALL* your heart and with *ALL* your mind." We are to lean, trust, and be confident in him!

"In all your ways, know, recognize and acknowledge him and he will direct [web: to bring from one point to another without deviation by the shortest way] and make straight and plain [web: unobstructed] your paths." (v. 6)

God is well aware that the enemy can and will strike us suddenly with fear and panic and warns us of this in the book of Proverbs.

Proverbs 3:25 and 26 states, "Be not afraid of sudden terror and panic, nor of the stormy blast or the storm and ruin of the wicked when it comes for you [for you will be guiltless]." (v. 25)

God says it's not your fault, so quit letting the enemy fill your mind with "there's something wrong with you"! He's a liar, was from the beginning, and always will be.

"For the Lord shall be your confidence, firm and strong and shall keep your foot from being caught [in a trap or some hidden danger]." (v. 26)

God does not want us to press through after we have calmed down or the storms have ceased, feeling relieved or for all conditions to be favorable, but rather in the midst of our attacks when all hell is coming against you. This is where we experience the true faithfulness of God and his almighty power.

Ecclesiastes 11:4 and 5 states, "He who observes the wind [and waits for all conditions to be favorable] will not sow [web: to set something in motion] and him who regards the clouds will not reap [web: obtain or win]." (v. 4)

God is speaking figuratively here. When a storm comes, there are clouds and winds. Many times in the Bible, God refers to trials or troubles as storms, and the clouds and winds are the effects of that storm (distress, worry, anxiety, fear, trembling, sickness etc).

God is telling us here not to observe (web: conform ones action) to the winds or effects of the storm or wait for everything to calm down but to press through in the midst of the storm.

"As you know not what is the way of the wind or how the spirit comes to the bones in the womb of a pregnant woman even so you know not the work of God, who does all." (v. 5)

The spirit of the Lord is what comes in trials, and it is *HE* who accomplishes what *HE* wills.

PLEASURE IN INFIRMITIES

The author Paul, who wrote the book of Corinthians, actually took pleasure in his trials because he knew the God we serve to be faithful.

2 Corinthians 12:10 states, "So for the sake of Christ, I am well pleased and take pleasure in infirmities [web: state of being weak of mind, will, or character] insults, hardships, persecutions, perplexities [web: puzzled, full of difficulty] and distresses [web: anguish of body or mind]; for when I am weak [in human strength], then am I [truly] strong [able, powerful in divine strength].

Paul obviously learned the lesson by experience that God is trying to teach us. He was being put under many trials; his faith tested, he endured the attacks of the enemy by putting his trust in God. God comforted and encouraged him every time to the point where Paul states that he was well pleased and actually took pleasure during his attacks. He knew by experience that the God we serve would give him divine strength, ability, and the comfort of knowing God was with him.

2 Corinthians 1:3 and 4 states, "Blessed be the God and Father of our Lord Jesus Christ, the father of sympathy [pity and mercy] and the God [who is the source] of every comfort [consolation and encouragement]." (v. 3)

"Who comforts [consoles and encourages] us in every trouble [calamity and affliction] so that we may also be able to comfort [console and encourage] those who are in any kind of trouble or distress, with the comfort with which we ourselves are comforted by God." (v. 4)

Don't you too want to get to this point as Paul did where you actually take pleasure in trials, excitedly awaiting to see God do his work with his Almighty Splendor? Where you actually see yourself running to battle instead of running from it? Then you *MUST* PRESS through in FAITH as he instructs!

Chapter
8

Don't Let Your Emotions Rule

KEEP YOUR EMOTIONS IN CHECK

The word *emotion*, as defined according to *Webster*, is "to move away, disturb, state of feeling psychic and physical reaction (as anger or fear) subjectively experienced as strong feeling and physiologically involving changes that prepare the body for immediate vigorous action."

Satan can and will attack your emotions to stop and hinder God's blessings and freedom in Christ. It is another avenue that he uses to keep you from being all you can be for God. He is always trying to thwart God's plan for you. Therefore, it is extremely important to *NOT* let your emotions rule you or base decisions upon them. They are unreliable. Remember, we walk by faith, not by sight or how we feel!

God says in his Word to keep our eyes and focus straight before us unto him, not looking to the right or to the left at the distraction of the enemy. Let's look at one of David's prayers.

Psalm 55:1–3 states, "Listen to my prayer, O God, and hide not yourself from my supplication [web: to ask for earnestly and humbly]! (v. 1)

"Attend to me and answer me: I am restless and distraught in my complaint and must moan." (v. 2)

"[And I am distracted] At the noise of the enemy, because of the oppression [web: crush or burden by abuse of power or authority, sense of being weighed down in body or mind] and threats of the wicked; for they would cast trouble upon me, and in wrath [web: strong vengeful anger] they persecute [cause to suffer because of belief, harass in a manner designed to injure, grieve, or afflict] me." (v. 3)

Please note, the first thing David did when his emotions were under attack was pray!

I can't stress enough how important this is. Run to God our Father and PRAY FIRST! Then in verse 3, we see the clue why he was feeling restless and distraught. He was distracted by the noise of the enemy. Satan loves to set up distractions to get us to take our eyes off our Father in hopes to rob us of the peace and joy God wants us to have always throughout our day. He is constantly scheming and planning to rip us off in any way he can, even through those around us if we allow. We have to be constantly watchful, recognizing why and from where these attacks are coming from. God gives us wisdom to help us in these times of troubles or trials in the book of Proverbs.

Proverbs 4:25–27 states, "Let your eyes look right on [with fixed purpose] and let your gaze be straight before you." (v. 25)

God is telling us to keep our focus upon Him and His Word and not on the noise or distractions of the enemy!

"Consider well the path of your feet and let all your ways be established [web: set on a firm basis] and ordered [web: marked by discipline] aright [web: correctly]." (v. 26)

"Turn not aside to the right hand or to the left, remove your foot from evil [web: something that brings sorrow, distress, or calamity]." (v. 27)

God says to keep our eyes (focus) on him at all times waiting for his instruction, carefully watching and considering the paths we take. Note in verse 27 where he says "remove your foot from evil".

Well, we must be able to do this or he wouldn't have said it. But how do we do this when evil presents itself from all sides? By not placing your thought and focus upon it. Satan loves to get our attention because it takes our focus off the Word and our God. The word *remove* is defined as "pushing aside, taking away or off".

Let all our ways be set on a firm basis of the Word, using discipline correctly. Don't let your focus or your thoughts turn to the right or to the left on the evil Satan is trying to attack you with. Keep your eyes straight before you, looking upon Jesus our Savior. Just keep pressing on, one foot in front of the other. Always remember, the battle belongs to God. Trust in and rely on him and he promises to bring you through.

AN ANXIOUS AND TROUBLED MIND

Jesus specifically addresses an anxious and troubled mind in the book of Luke.

Luke 12:22–24 states, "And [Jesus] said to his disciples, 'Therefore, I tell you, do not be anxious [web: characterized by extreme uneasiness of mind or brooding fear about something possible but uncertain occurrence) and troubled [web: agitate mentally or spiritually, worry, disturb with cares] about your life, as to what you will eat or about your body, as to what you will wear." (v. 22)

"For life is more than food, and the body is more than clothes." (v. 23)

"Observe and consider the ravens, for they neither sow nor reap, they have neither storehouse nor barn and [yet] God feeds them. Of how much more worth are you than the birds!" (v. 24)

Jesus is telling us to not worry about anything, for it is God who is our sufficiency. He takes care of the birds, so why wouldn't he take care of us who are more important to him than the birds. He continues speaking.

Luke 22:32 states, "Do not be seized with alarm and struck with fear, little flock, for it is your Fathers good pleasure to give you the Kingdom!"

Many times, I've noticed when the devil comes and attacks me emotionally, he presents the question to my mind. "Well, what are you going to do now?" Well, we can answer back with the Word. "I will walk by faith, I will not fear, God will take care of me!" God eagerly wants to give us all things!

I can remember something the Lord gave me during my painstaking attacks of fear and panic. He said, "I want you to quit worrying about tomorrow and enjoy what I am giving you today. I will give you what you need for today and not for tomorrow. And when tomorrow comes, I will give you what you need then."

Satan loves to attack your mind with worries about your life in the future. What if I can't find a job? What if I lose my job? What if I never find that special someone? What if I never get over this anxiety? What if I get sick? What if, what if, what if! And his biggest one is this: What if God doesn't come through? Quit listening to him and his lies! God says to *TRUST IN HIM!*

Matthew 6:34 states, "So do not worry or be anxious about tomorrow, for tomorrow will have worries and anxieties of its own. Sufficient [web: enough to meet the needs of a situation] for each day is its own trouble [web: agitate mentally or spiritually]."

So quit worrying about your tomorrows. How are you going to make it, what will you do? God is our sufficiency and does not want us to worry about *ANYTHING!*

2 Corinthians 3:5 states, "Not that we are fit [qualified and sufficient in ability] of ourselves to form personal judgments or to claim or count anything as coming from us, but our power and ability and sufficiency are from God."

We either make the choice during trials to let Satan's power rule over us by giving in to fear and panic or let God's power reign over us by giving it to God, walking in absolute trust and faith that he will take care of us as he promises to do so in the Word.

What Will You Choose?

Write down some examples of what you're struggling with to walk by faith in, rather than letting fear stop you:

WALK BY EMOTIONS OR WALK BY FAITH?

**What will you choose?
Walk by Emotions or by Faith?**

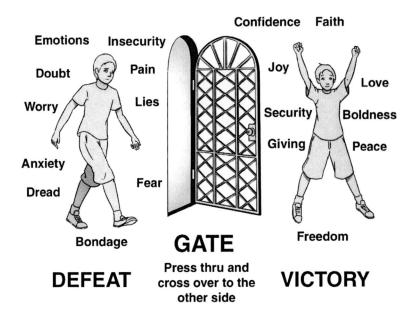

If you really want to be set free in your life, then you must follow GOD'S INSTRUCTION PLAN that he sets forth in his Word. God tells us to submit to his Word, obey, and we shall see results.

Proverbs 4:20–22 states, "My son, attend [web: apply the mind or pay attention to as with a companion] to my words, consent [web: be in compliance] and submit to my sayings." (v. 20)

"Let them not depart from your sight, keep them in the center of your heart." (v. 21)

"For they are life to those who find them, healing and health to all their flesh." (v. 22)

These are some very important instructions God gives us here in the book of Proverbs to achieve the promise of healing and health to all our flesh. In verse 20, God says to apply the mind and to give attention to his words as a companion or associate. Then, he says, to consent (web: be in compliance to what he says) and also submit (web: to yield oneself to the authority or will of another). So this is his first instruction to us that precedes his promise of healing and health.

Then, in verse 21, He says not to let His words depart (web: turn aside or go away or deviate from our sight). In other words, he wants our focus to be on his Word, always, keeping them in the center (web: a point of utmost importance) of our heart (web: one's innermost character, feelings, or inclinations). Then comes the promise.

Still talking about his Word (the Bible), that they are life (web: a way or manner of living) to those who find (web: come upon by searching) them, healing (web: to make sound or whole) and health (web: the condition of being sound in body, mind or spirit; freedom from physical disease or pain) to all their flesh.

Note how God says his words are life to all those who find them. How do we find something is by searching. God wants us to search the scriptures *DAILY!* God is amazing and how lovingly he provides for us victory over each and everything that troubles us if we simply obey. The Bible is indeed God's instruction plan for us all as to how to live this life while we are here in this world.

Proverbs 4:1 and 2 states, "Hear my sons, the instruction of a father and pay attention in order to gain and to know intelligent discernment, comprehension and interpretation [of spiritual matters]." (v. 1)

"For I give you good doctrine [web: instruction]; do not forsake [web: quit or withdraw from] my teaching." (v. 2)

Satan wants to hold you back in fear and past experiences, but God wants to give you victory by pressing through to the new, to the joy he has waiting for you. Jesus gave his life to not leave us powerless! Press on to what God has for you.

KEEP PRESSING ON

While Paul was in prison, he was inspired by God and wrote more of these instructions in the book of Philippians.

Philippians 3:10, 13 and 14 states, "[For my determined purpose is] That I may know him [that I may progressively become more deeply and intimately acquainted with him, perceiving and recognizing and understanding the wonders of his person more strongly and more clearly], and that I may in that same way come to know the power outflowing from his [Jesus'] resurrection [which exerts over believers] and that I may so share his sufferings as to be continually transformed [in spirit into his likeness even] to his death [in the hope]." (v. 10)

"I do not consider brethren, that I have captured and made it my own [yet] but one thing I do [it is my one aspiration] forgetting what lies behind and straining forward to what lies ahead." (v. 13)

"I press on toward the goal to win the [supreme and heavenly] prize to which God in Christ is calling us upward." (v. 14)

Even Paul knew he had to keep pressing on toward the goal to win the spiritual battles we all face. The word *press*, according to *Webster*, is "to follow through with a course of action". Sometimes, it takes a lot of pressing through to get through each day, but yet this is what God says to do when under attack. Don't settle for what's comfortable to you but rather press through when all hell is coming against you. This opens the door for power and victory. Pray and ask God to give you the courage and strength you need to press through trials. Don't allow for a second to let the enemy trick you in condemning yourself or to think something's wrong with you. Remember, God says, "He is a liar!" You are more than a conqueror in Christ!

No matter how long you may have been going through these attacks of fear and panic. feeling your situation is hopeless, perhaps even been on medication or other means to cope for years, *GOD STILL CAN AND WILL DELIVER YOU* if you ask him and begin to seek him as your vital necessity and then follow his instructions that he sets forth in his Word. He will open your eyes of understanding so that you can begin to see more clearly in understanding why you're going through this, and thus begin the road to freedom that he desires for you to have. Always remember: It is a spiritual battle you're facing!

The devil, our enemy, may have stolen much from you over the years, but God is in the business of restoration to give you back everything the enemy stole and more.

Joel 2:25 and 26 states, "And I will restore or replace for you the years that the locust has eaten-the hopping locust, the stripping locust and the crawling locust, My great army which I sent among you." (v. 25)

As I read this verse, I wondered about the ladder part where it says "My great army which I sent among you." I then prayed and asked the Lord, why he would send anything uncomfortable our way. He answered and told me that he desires that we be stripped of our old ways of thinking and doing so that we will have no choice but to look to him. This is why he allows certain things to befall us! As long as we still depend on ourselves and our own abilities, we will fight a losing battle against our enemy because we cannot fight the spiritual battles in our flesh. God knows this, and this is why he needs to strip off the dependency we all have of our own strengths and abilities. But the sooner we adhere to the truths of his Word, the quicker we shall see the deliverance of the Lord.

What kind of Father would he be if he just left us defenseless, knowing we could never win? *NO* He loves us so much and allows things in our lives to get our attention so that we will make the choice to look to him for answers. Because he knows there and only there is where we will find freedom and live the blessed life. And when we do make that choice, HE not only delivers but gives us back everything the enemy stole.

"And you shall eat in plenty and be satisfied and praise the name of our Lord, your God who has dealt wondrously with you. And my people shall never be put to shame." (v. 26)

Isaiah 61:7 states, "Instead of your [former] shame, you shall have a twofold recompense [web: to give something by way of compensation]; instead of dishonor [web: lack or loss of reputation, rather die than live in] and reproach [web: discredit or disgrace] your people shall rejoice in their portion. Therefore, in their land they shall possess double [what they had forfeited]; everlasting joy shall be theirs."

How many times, when being struck by these attacks, have you felt like you are disgraced and your reputation has been lost, leaving you feeling like you would rather die than live? Well, God promises that if you adhere to his Word, he will not only turn everything around for us when we adhere to his Word, but he will also compensate us double for everything the enemy stole. Jesus spoke of this abundant life in the book of John.

John 10:10 states, "The thief comes only in order to steal, kill and destroy, I came that they may have and enjoy life and have it in abundance to the full, till it overflows."

Jesus is telling us here that Satan, our enemy, is out to steal, kill, and destroy. This is his plan, but Jesus came that we overcome Satan's plan by giving us a more than abundant life in him and left us a way or instructions as to how to achieve this life of abundance.

Jeremiah 30:16 and 17 states, "Therefore all who devour [web: to seize upon and destroy, to prey upon a man by guilt] you will be devoured, all your adversaries, everyone of them will go into captivity. And they who despoil [web: strip of belongings, possessions or value] you will become a spoil and all who prey [web: to commit violence, robbery, or fraud] upon you will I give for a prey [web: one that is helpless or unable to resist attack]." (v. 16)

"For I will restore health to you and I will heal your wounds says the Lord because they have called you an outcast saying, This is Zion, whom no one seeks after and for whom no one cares!" (v. 17)

God is on our side and is always there, in favor of those who belong to Him, *US!*

Every day, you must try to regain the territory the enemy has stolen from you, even if it's only little by little. Always lean on God's instruction plan and on his grace and not on your own ability to achieve victory.

GOD PROMISES

God gives us many promises in his Word to let us know that he is indeed with us during troubles or our enemies' attacks and promises to help us when we look to him and rely on him.

Isaiah 43:2 states, "When you pass through the waters [troubles of any kind], I will be with you and through the rivers, they will not overwhelm you. When you walk through the fire, you will not be burned or scorched, nor will the flame kindle upon you."

Psalm 23:3 and 4 states, "He refreshes [web: restores strength, maintain by renewing supply; replenish] and restores [web: to bring back to or put back into former or original state; renew] my life [myself]; He leads me in the paths of righteousness [uprightness and right standing with him, not for my earning it, but] for his names sake." (v. 3)

"Yes, though I walk through the [deep, sunless] valley of the shadow of death, I will fear or dread no evil, for you are with me; your rod [to protect] and your staff [to guide] they comfort me." (v. 4)

2 Timothy 1:7 and 8 states, "For God did not give us a spirit of timidity [of cowardice, of craven and cringing and fawning fear], but [he has given us a spirit] of power and of love and of a calm and well balanced mind and discipline and self control." (v. 7)

"Do not blush or be ashamed then to testify to and for our Lord nor of me [speaking of Paul] take your share of the suffering [to which the preaching] of the Gospel [may expose you and do it] in the power of God." (v. 8)

Fawning fear is a fear that makes you want to cower and run.

Every day as you study and search the scriptures more, you will begin to grow much closer to God, and *HE WILL* reveal more and more truths to you—the truth that will set you free! He will form you into being more Christlike as he reveals to us in Isaiah, where he states he is the Potter, and we are the clay. He is the one who forms us.

Isaiah 64:8 states, "Yet, O Lord, You are our Father, we are the clay and you are our Potter and we are all the work of your hand."

God is the Potter

US

God is forming and shaping us everyday.

CHECK YOUR EMOTIONS AND YOUR THOUGHTS

Live in the SPIRIT and not in the flesh:
(Members warring against one another)

Flesh:	Versus:	Spirit:
Anger		Confidence
Pride	(Check your emotions	Love
Complaining	and thoughts:	Giving
Worry, Fear	Everything starts here)	Encourage
Doubt	Patience	Trust in God
Depression	Faith	
Impatience	Endurance	

Your flesh and your spirit are at constant war against one another. The flesh wills what it wills, but the spirit brings everlasting joy and truth to us; therefore, we need to live in the spirit and *not* in the flesh.

Romans 7:23–25 states, "But I discern in my bodily members [in the sensitive appetites and wills of the flesh] a different law [rule of action] at war against the law of my mind [my reason] and making me a prisoner to the law of sin that dwells in my bodily organs [in the sensitive appetites and wills of the flesh]." (v. 23)

"O unhappy and pitiable and wretched man that I am! Who will release and deliver me from [the shackles of] this body of death?" (v. 24)

"O thank God! [He will!] through Jesus Christ [the Anointed One] our Lord! So then indeed I, of myself with the mind and heart, serve the Law of God, but with the flesh, the law of sin." (v. 25)

Galatians 5:17 states, "For the desires of the flesh are opposed to the [Holy] Spirit and the [desires of the] Spirit are opposed to the flesh [godless human nature]; for these are antagonistic to each other [continually withstanding and in conflict with each other] so that you are not free but are prevented from doing what you desire to do."

Therefore, God makes it clear we are not to live in the flesh, but rather live in the Spirit. The only way to do this is to do what the Word says rather than what our flesh dictates.

Prayer:

Father, help me win the battle in my flesh and teach me to live in the Spirit. Strengthen me to have the mind of Christ in each and every situation and trial that comes my way, so that I can better serve you with a humble, loving spirit. In the name of Jesus Christ, amen!

Chapter
9

Know Who You Are and Stay Strong

God is well aware of the pain you're going through and of the torment the enemy tempts you with. He has addressed this very issue many times in his Word and gives us the power to overcome each and every battle if we just believe.

GODS GREATEST DESIRE AND JOY

God's greatest desire above all things is found in the third book of John.

3 John 1:2 states, "Beloved, I wish above all things that thou mayest prosper and be in health even as thy soul prospereth." (KJV)

Note here how God addresses us as beloved or dearly loved. He loves us much more than we can comprehend, and it is very important for us to realize this as it is also a key to freedom. So many of us go on through life feeling so empty and unloved, and it greatly hinders our success in more ways than we realize. Many people go searching their whole lives, looking for that love to complete them, and if we don't find that love, we somehow feel like we failed. Well, when you really come to the knowledge of how much God Loves You, you can feel complete in him; and our natural relationship with a man or woman becomes second to him in addition, but our main source is that of God. As you begin to diligently study God's Word in depth, making it your aim and goal to get to know him better and become more deeply acquainted with him, you will indeed perceive more clearly how much he really loves you!

Definitions for Greek Words for Love in the Bible:

- Agapeo or (Agape): Unconditional love; the love of God. God's love for us is not dependent upon circumstances or what we do for him. He simply loves us unconditionally. Nothing can ever separate us from this love.

Romans 8:38 and 39 states, "For I am persuaded beyond doubt [am sure] that neither death nor life, nor angels or principalities, nor things impending and threatening nor things to come, nor powers," (v. 38)

"Nor height nor depth, nor anything else in all creation will be able to separate us from the love of God which is in Christ Jesus our Lord. (v. 39)

- Phileo: Love between friends
- Eros: The sense of being in love; romantic love
- Storge: Love of family; Parent/child, siblings, cousins, etc. (In a very close family, agape is felt as well)

Many people today think of love as being a feeling, but this is not true of agape love. Agape is love because of what it does, not because of how it feels; John 3:16 states, "For God so loved [agape] the world that he gave his only son."

Of course, it did not feel good for God to do this, but it was out of his love for us that he did it.

Sometimes in life, we may pray for someone sick, and they die; and we wonder where God's love is here? But we cannot question this, for God has a plan and purpose for all he does; and it is many times out of our realm of understanding. Just as he let Jesus die even though he did not feel good about it, yet he had a purpose that benefited all mankind! Someday we will come to understand all things, but for now, we need to trust that God knows what he's doing.

Gods greatest joy is found in the amplified version.

3 John 1:4 states, "I have no greater joy than this, to hear that my [spiritual] children are living their lives in the truth."

Why? Because God knows here and only here is where we find that freedom and victory over our enemy (Satan), therefore bringing us the life he desires for us all to have.

God has no greater joy than to see us, his children, not just knowing the truth (which is his Word) but that we are also living or walking our lives in the truth. I've heard a pastor say one time, "A stick of dynamite has a lot of power, but until you light it, it has no effect." Well, this is true for God's Word; we have to live it. And then, we shall see the power of God released and manifested in our lives.

Prayer:

Lord, I come to you, asking that you restore my soul and have my soul prosper. As you say, this is what you desire as well. Show me how to do this, having no anxieties or worries about anything anymore but fully trusting you for *all* things. Show me how to achieve the more than abundant life you have planned for me. In Jesus's name, amen!

Jesus said the thief or our enemy, Satan, comes only to bring havoc in our lives, but he (Jesus) came that we may have a more than abundant life.

John 10:10 states "The thief comes only in order to steal, kill, and destroy, I came that they may have and enjoy life and have it in abundance [to the fullest, till it overflows]."

You don't have to worry or fear about anything. Simply believe, receive his love, and the blessings he longs to give you as promised in his Word will be yours. Remember, God wants to give you all the desires of your heart!

SEE YOURSELF THE WAY GOD SEES YOU

Satan loves to see us, God's children, live in constant condemnation (web: state of being wrong or evil, be sentenced or doomed). He knows if he can keep you in this state of mind, he has the victory. But God tells us not to feel this way in the book of Romans.

Romans 8:1 states, "Therefore, [there is] now no condemnation [no adjudging, guilty of wrong] for those who are in Christ Jesus, who live [and] walk not after the dictates of the flesh but after the dictates of the spirit."

God does not want us living this life being bogged down by looking or walking in this flesh, focusing on everything that's wrong with us, but rather looking to God, our creator, and seeing everything he did for us that made us right before him.

Romans 8:28–31 states, "We are assured and know that [God being a partner in their labor] all things work together and are [fitting into a plan] for good and for those who love God and are called according to [his] design and purpose." (v. 28)

"For those whom he foreknew [of whom he was aware and loved beforehand], He also destined from the beginning [fore-ordaining them] to be molded into the image of his Son [and share inwardly His likeness), that he might become the first born among many brethren." (v. 29)

"And those whom he thus fore-ordained, He also called; and those whom he called, He also justified [acquitted, made righteous, putting them in right standing with himself]. And those whom he justified, he also glorified [raising them to a heavenly dignity and condition or state of being]." (v. 30)

Let's look more closely at this verse where we find four very important things God did for us:

1. God actually fore-ordained us which, according to *Webster*, means "to order or appoint with ministerial or priestly authority".
2. God called us or summoned, caused us to come to him.
3. He also justified, proved to, or showed us to be just or right. Just as if we never sinned.
4. He also glorified us, bestowing honor, praise or admiration. Wow! God actually honors, praises, and admires US!

This is the way God wants us to see ourselves!

"What then shall we say to [all] this? If God be for us, who [can be] against us? [Who can be our foe if God is on our side?]." (v. 31)

THROUGH AND WITH JESUS, WE ARE
MORE THAN CONQUERORS!

Let's continue on in the book of Romans.

Romans 8:32–37 states, "He who did not withhold or spare [even] his own Son but gave him up for us all, will he not also with him freely and graciously give us all things?" (v. 32)

"Who shall bring any charge to Gods elect [when it is] God who justifies. That is, who puts us in right relation to himself? Who shall come forward and accuse or impeach [web: to bring an accusation against] those whom God has chosen? Will God who acquits us?" (v. 33)

"Who is there to condemn [us]? Will Christ Jesus [the Messiah] who died or rather who was raised from the dead, Who is at the right hand of God actually pleading as he intercedes [web: to intervene between parties with a view to reconciling differences, mediate] for us?" (v. 34)

Jesus actually sits at the right hand of God, as our defense attorney so to speak. He was attacked by the devil in every aspect of life far beyond what you or I will ever have to endure while being in the flesh. He was here on this earth and therefore knows and understands every weakness of the flesh and every assault of our enemy the devil.

Hebrews 4:14–16 states, "Inasmuch, then as we have a great High Priest who has [already] ascended and passed through the heavens, Jesus the Son of God, let us hold fast our confession [of faith] in him." (v. 14)

"For we do not have a High Priest [Jesus] who is unable to understand and sympathize and have a shared feeling with our weaknesses and infirmities [web: condition of being weak of mind, will, or character] and liability to the assaults of temptation, but one who has been tempted in every respect as we are, yet without sinning." (v. 15)

"Let us then fearlessly and confidently and boldly draw near to the throne of grace [the throne of God's unmerited favor to us, sinners] that we may receive mercy [for our failures] and find grace to help in good time for every need [appropriate help and well-timed help, coming just when we need it]." (v. 16)

God wants us to approach the throne of grace in all confidence without fear, knowing that his mercy and grace will give us the help we need! Let's return to the book of Romans.

Romans 8:35 & 36 states, "Who shall ever separate us from Christ's love? Shall suffering and affliction and tribulation? Or calamity and distress? Or persecution or hunger or destitution or peril or sword?"

"Even as it is written, For thy sake, we are put to death all the day long; we are regarded and counted as sheep for the slaughter." (v. 36)

In verses 35 and 36, are all things our enemy the devil presents. But in verse 37, it states, "Yet amid all these things, we are more than conquerors [web: to gain mastery over or win by overcoming obstacles or opposition] and gain a surpassing [web: greatly exceeding others] victory [web: the overcoming of an enemy; achievement of mastery or success in a struggle against odds or difficulties] through him who loved us."

God doesn't just say here that we are conquerors but more than conquerors! He has equipped you and I to be victorious over each and every battle the enemy tempts us with. Remember Always, the devil is a liar! Don't believe what he whispers in your ear but believe what God is telling you in his Word!

JESUS LEFT US INSTRUCTIONS

Before Jesus ascended up to heaven, He told us not to be fearful or intimidated of our enemy but to rely on him for help in everything. He said these words to us in the book of John.

John 14:27–29 states, "Peace I leave with you. My [own] peace I now give and bequeath [web: to give or leave by will, to hand down to you], Do not let your hearts be troubled, neither let them be afraid. [Stop allowing yourselves to be agitated and disturbed, and do not permit yourselves to be fearful and intimidated and cowardly and unsettled]." (v. 27)

"You have heard me tell you, I am going away and I am coming [back] to you. If you [really] loved me, you would have been glad; because I am going to the Father; for the Father is greater and mightier than I am." (v. 28)

Jesus is telling us here that even though he was leaving them in the physical realm, he is going to return here once again. We need to be ready for his return by doing those things that he instructs us to do through the Word!

"And now I have told you [this] before it occurs so that when it does take place, you may believe and have faith in and rely on me." (v. 29)

Jesus tells us here to stop being troubled and fearful about anything but to rely on *HIM* always to take care of anything that comes our way in *FAITH, BELIEVING*.

If this was an impossible thing to do, he wouldn't have told us to do it. Therefore, it must be possible to stop being troubled and fearful. The devil is the one who keeps whispering in your ear, "I can't help worrying and being afraid." Quit listening to him, remembering he is all lies and BELIEVE the truth of the Word! Jesus tells us that he is always with us and that we are never alone.

Matthew 28:20b states, "I am with you all the days [perpetually, uniformly and on every occasion], to the [very] close and consummation [web: the ultimate end, finish] of the age."

We can depend on him always, and he will never leave us!

In the beginning, when God began dealing with me in this area of fear and panic, I can recall many mornings awakened by this awful nauseous feeling in my stomach that would come and go throughout the day. Satan had been attacking me with accusations of things I wasn't doing when I was trying to give God's love and help other people. I found the people I was trying to help were the ones the enemy was using to attack me. The devil can and will work through those around you, and even family is no exception! I can remember one day, I was helping someone by giving them a ride, and they physically attacked me in my car while I was driving. I had been under a huge amount of pressure and stress with the enemy waging total war against me. I kept replacing the negative thoughts and situations with the Word of God in continual prayer.

I just felt like staying in my house, keeping the door shut and being by myself, but God told me to go out and do some things I enjoy. It helped me to get my mind off things that were troubling me. Still, nausea and feelings of anxiety kept taunting me throughout the day. I kept looking to God to give me strength, confidence, and boldness to get me through the day; and each time, I could feel his peace coming over me when Satan kept trying to hit me with his annoying, persistent attacks. But each time, God was there, and I could feel his strength and peace giving me power to endure.

A lot of the attacks seemed to be more severe at night, when I was headed to sleep when I was really tired. It was like this wave of anxious thoughts trying to overtake me so I couldn't get any rest. I decided in those times to read, study, and pray before going to sleep. And the key word here is STUDY! I didn't just read scripture, I literally studied it for hours.

I actually remember, during those times, telling the devil, "If you are going to try to keep me up all night with these attacks, then I will use the time to get closer to my Lord and study his Word." And I did just that!

Then he tried to hit my mind with the question, "Well, you have to work tomorrow and how will you do that with no sleep?" And I would answer back with scripture, "I can do all things through Christ who gives me strength." God also reminded me that without him, I could do nothing and that with him, I can do anything if I stay in union with him.

Many nights after studying for hours, I would drift off for an hour or so, only to find myself waking up in a total state of panic—sweating, trembling, and heart racing for no apparent reason. God would remind me night after night that instead of lying there, thinking about what I was going through, to get up, seek him, pray, and get right back into his Word. This is spiritual warfare! I obeyed his voice and pleaded with him to take the anxiety away that Satan was attacking me with. Each and every time, within thirty minutes, all anxieties fled and God's peace came over me. God had indeed been showing me that I was in a great spiritual battle. How could my whole being be in such great torment and then after reading, studying, and praying for thirty minutes, feel a wave of total calming peace flow through me? Because, believer, there is power in the Word of God, power that we cannot see. This is something the Lord wanted to show me by experience, and therefore, I could share with you as well. The more you read and study his Word, the more power you will experience and that of God. God is a God of great mighty power and *HE CAN* do anything, but we need to follow his instructions as found in his Word.

DON'T GET WEARY OR FRUSTRATED

During my battle, I could feel myself getting discouraged at times even though I was receiving breakthroughs and God had given me victory when I chose to walk by faith and keep pressing through trials. I told God, "It's so hard being a Christian!" It was the daily constant battle that was wearing me out, those nagging negative thoughts the enemy kept whispering in my ear relentlessly day after day. I started to get weary with the feeling of this spiritual battle, waging constant war inside me! All I wanted was *PEACE!* I then prayed to the Lord, "I know you always deliver me when I don't allow these emotions to stop me from doing the things I need to do, but I want peace beforehand." Then the Lord spoke to my heart and said, "Don't waver or get weary in the battle of your mind. I will bring you through. Remember, your prayer is to live without any fear. This is a huge goal and don't think Satan is simply going to step aside and give up so easily. He will try to intimidate you with great storms but set your face like flint and be determined to stay in faith regardless of how you feel or how circumstances present themselves. Remember, breakthroughs come as you keep pressing through in faith."

Isaiah 50:7 states, "For the Lord helps Me; therefore have I not been ashamed or confounded [web: confused or full of difficulty]. Therefore, have I set my face like flint [not shrink from any degree of suffering, firm, resolute] and know that I shall not be put to shame."

One day, the Lord also brought to my attention my little dog whom I've had for years. Everywhere I go, he follows me. If I leave the room, he follows; outside, he follows; from one chair to the next, he follows; if I start to leave the house to head for my car, he follows and begs to come. The Lord told me to look at him (my dog) and said, "Do you see how your dog constantly sticks closely to you? He never leaves your side! This is how I want you to be with me." I will never forget that day, and he is a constant reminder to always stay close to God. He is closer than our next breath.

We have to constantly remember that the battle is not ours to fight but the Lords, and he promises to help, strengthen, and give us his peace when we obey his Word. I can do all things through Christ who gives me strength!

In the book of Isaiah, God tells us exactly what to do when we are in darkness and in deep trouble.

Isaiah 50:10 states, "Who is among you who [reverently] fears the Lord, who obeys the voice of his servant, yet who walks in darkness and deep trouble and has no shinning splendor [in his heart]? Let him rely on, trust in and be confident in the name of the Lord and let him lean upon and be supported by his God."

During my trials of fear and panic, I asked God, why? "Why am I going through this? I know by your hand, you can deliver me right now." It's okay to ask God, why. He is our closest friend, companion, and Father and wants to reveal his truths to us. He answered and said, "I want you to seek me more in your life and not be so dependent on yourself or others but solely and completely dependent upon me." He then led me to the second book of Corinthians.

2 Corinthians 12:7–10 states, "And to keep me from being too puffed up and too much elated [web: prideful] by the exceeding greatness [pre-eminince] of these revelations, there was given me a thorn [a splinter] in the flesh, a messenger of Satan, to rack [web: to cause to suffer torture, pain, or anguish] and buffet [web: strike repeatedly] and harass [web: to worry and interfere with or slow the progress of by repeated raids of the enemy] me, to keep me from being excessively exalted [web: to raise in rank, power or character]." (v. 7)

"Three times, I called upon the Lord and besought [him] about this and begged that it might depart from me." (v. 8)

"But he said to me, my grace [my favor and loving kindness and mercy] is enough for you [sufficient against any danger and enables you to bear the trouble manfully]: for my strength and power, are made perfect [fulfilled, completed] and show themselves most effective in [your] weakness. Therefore, I will all the more gladly glory [web: worshipful praise, honor, and thanksgiving to God] in my weaknesses and infirmities [web: personal failings, frailties] that the strength and power of Christ [the Messiah] may rest [yes, may pitch a tent over and dwell] upon me!" (v. 9)

"So for the sake of Christ, I am well pleased and take pleasure in infirmities insults, hardships, persecutions, perplexities [web: full of difficulties] and distresses; for when I am weak [in human strength] then am I [truly] strong [able, powerful in divine strength]." (v. 10)

Many people have wondered just what the thorn in Paul's side was but the Bible does not reveal it. But we can indeed be sure that it was an attack of the enemy that God did allow to affect Paul. I've often wondered if it could be this attack of fear and panic. We just don't know for sure but can only speculate.

It is only natural in our sinful human flesh to have the tendency to become puffed up or prideful as God begins to unfold his truths to us. God, our Father, does not want us to do this but rather wants us to receive his truths and secrets in his Word with all meekness and humbleness and not to place ourselves in higher positions over others. We should rather pray that God would enlighten or open the eyes of others to see and understand the truth that will set them free as well.

GOD CORRECTS THOSE HE LOVES

This is why we need that discipline and correction from the Lord because the Bible tells us that in our flesh dwells no good thing!

Romans 7:18 states. "For I know that nothing good dwells within me, that is in my flesh. I can will what is right, but I cannot perform it. [I have the intention and urge to do what is right but no power to carry it out]."

That is why we need the Holy Spirit that dwells within us to give us the power and strength to do God's will.

Hebrews 12:6–11 states, "For the Lord corrects and disciplines everyone whom he loves and punishes even scourges [web: subject to affliction] every son whom he accepts and welcomes to his heart." (v. 6)

"You must subject to and endure [correction] for discipline; God is dealing with you as sons [or daughters]. For what son is there whom his father does not [thus] train and correct and discipline?" (v. 7)

"Now if you are exempt from correction and left without discipline in which all of God's children] share, then you are illegitimate offspring and not true sons [at all]." (v. 8)

"Moreover, we have had earthly fathers who disciplined us and we yielded [to them] and respected [them for training us]. Shall we not much more cheerfully submit to the Father of Spirits and so [truly] live?" (v. 9)

"For [our earthly fathers] disciplined us only for a short period of time and chastised us as seemed proper and good to them; but he [God] disciplines us for our certain good, that we may become sharers in his own holiness." (v. 10)

"For the time no discipline brings joy, but seems grievous and painful but afterwards it yields a peaceable fruit of righteousness to those who have been trained by it." (v. 11)

To get a clearer meaning of this verse, let's read this same verse from the English Standard Version.

Hebrews 12:11 states, "For the moment all discipline seems painful rather than pleasant, but later it yields the peaceful fruit of righteousness to those who have been trained by it." (ESV)

I want to emphasize, believer, that God does not enjoy chastising us but wants to correct us in the right way of thinking and doing because this is the *only* way to receive the joy and peaceable freedom he longs to give us.

We get so caught up in our flesh and things the world has taught us that we need to be retrained in our ways of thinking and doing. And how can we do this if we don't receive right correction? The only way to receive right correction is through God's Word!

GOD CORRECTS AND GIVES WISDOM

Proverbs 3:12–14 states, "For whom the Lord loves, he corrects, even as a father corrects the son in whom he delights." (v. 12)

"Happy [blessed, fortunate, enviable] is the man who finds skillful and godly wisdom and the man who gets understanding [drawing it forth from God's Word and life's experiences]." (v. 13)

Here, God denotes that if you want to find true happiness in your life, then you must find and use the wisdom that he provides us through his Word and study it which will bring forth understanding.

"For the gaining of it is better than the gaining of silver and the profit of it better than fine gold." (v. 14)

God is telling us here that this wisdom he provides is better than riches! God corrects those who he dearly loves, US!

Revelation 3:19 states, "Those whom I dearly and tenderly love, I tell their faults and convict and convince and reprove and chasten [I discipline and instruct them]. So be enthusiastic and in earnest and burning with zeal [web: eagerness and ardent interest in pursuit of something] and repent [changing your mind and attitude]."

God wants us to burn with eagerness and interest in him and in those things he wants to show us in his Word!

Think about something that you eagerly pursue and have that same attitude with the things of God.

NEVER A HOPELESS CASE FOR GOD

You may be thinking that you didn't have a mother or father who trained or instructed you as a child. Perhaps you were neglected, abused, or even abandoned which led you to a very destructive life filled with drug, alcohol, or eating disorder. Maybe you even chose a life getting involved in pornography, theft, or even murder.

Well, let me tell you, believer, that God still loves you; and if you choose to heed his instruction, he can set you free from anything that entangles, binds, or causes destruction in your life—no matter what the circumstance! Don't ever feel you are out of God's reach or your life is irreparable. There is nothing impossible for God!

The book of Isaiah speaks of those who live an entangled life of one in bondage.

Isaiah 61:1 states, "The spirit of the Lord is upon me, because the Lord has anointed and qualified me to preach the Gospel of good tidings to the meek, the poor and the afflicted; He has sent me to bind up and heal the broken hearted, to proclaim liberty to the [physical and spiritual] captives and the opening of the prison and of the eyes to those who are bound."

You are *NEVER* a hopeless case for our God! Satan is the one who has been injecting those negative thoughts in your mind for years.

Revelation 12:9 states, "And the huge dragon was cast down and out that age old serpent, who is called the devil and Satan, he is the seducer [deceiver] of all humanity the world over; he was forced out and down to the earth and his angels [those who chose to follow him] were flung out along with him."

Satan has been the one all the while, tricking your mind to believe all his lies; but now, it's time to recognize and see him for who he really is and believe the truth that God is revealing to you through his Word. God's desire is to set you free from his (Satan's) grip.

The simple fact is, we act and do according to what thoughts we entertain in our minds. Our enemy, the devil, is more than happy to be constantly injecting our minds with his evil thoughts, accusations, and intentions if we allow him to. Until you come to know this secret of truth that God sets forth for our knowledge in his Word and make the decision to occupy your mind with the thoughts of God's Word, you will never be truly free. The Word provides thoughts of love, peace, and confidence in our God that will transform your mind into right thinking and doing. This is contrary to what you have been taught by the world's standards. Paul speaks of not living by the customs of this world but rather changing your thinking to the standards of the Word.

Romans 12:2 states, "Do not be conformed [web: to be obedient, to adapt oneself to prevailing standards or customs] to this world [this age] but be transformed [changed] by the entire renewal of your mind [by its new ideals and its new attitude], so that you may prove [for yourselves] what is the good and acceptable and perfect will of God, even the thing which is good and acceptable and perfect [in his sight for you].

This is why God corrects us and disciplines us. It is for our joy, satisfaction, and freedom.

How can you know something unless you are taught? You have to ask yourself, do you want to be influenced by the enemy, Satan, whose only goal is to bring discouragement and destruction? Or do you want to be led and influenced by God who has your best interest at heart, bringing you joy, peace, and everlasting life? Only you can choose.

Jesus told Paul in the book of Acts that he wanted the people to be released from Satan's power and hold.

Acts 26:18 states, "To open their eyes that they may turn from darkness to light and from the power of Satan to God, so that they may receive forgiveness and release from their sins and a place and portion among those who are consecrated [web: to devote irrevocably to the worship of God], and purified by faith in me."

Even though your earthly parents may not have been there for you or have forgotten you, God says "he will never forget you."

Isaiah 49:15 and 16 states, "Can a woman forget her nursing child, that she should not have compassion on the son of her womb? Yes, they may forget, yet I will never forget you." (v. 15)

"Behold, I have indelibly [web: that which cannot be removed, washed away, or erased] imprinted [tattooed a picture of you] on the palm of each of my hands; your walls are continually before me." (v. 16)

The Love of God greatly surpasses that of a mother or father; have faith in that Love!

Chapter
10

Running on God's Srength

COME TO CHRIST AS A CHILD

During my trials of fear and panic, I can recall many mornings waking up with these nagging negative waves of anxious thoughts and asked the Lord what to do. I asked him to teach me how to live more in the spirit and not in the flesh. God replied, "Don't live and act by how you feel but rather in faith, lean on and trust me for everything!" Wow! *EVERYTHING*, I thought. "Yes, like a little child," he said. Then, he led me to a verse of scripture in the book of Luke.

Luke 18:17 states, "Truly I say to you, whoever does not accept and receive and welcome the Kingdom of God like a little child [does] shall not in any way enter it [at all]."

If you want to enter in the kingdom life here on this earth, you must be as a little child, simply believing and trusting God for EVERYTHING!

Think of a little baby after it's born. Babies don't go into a state of fear and panic, worrying whether or not they are going to be fed or have their needs taken care of. They simply trust that they will be. This is the way God wants us to be, to have the simplicity of a child's trust, believing that *HE* will take care of us, no matter what comes our way.

I have been self-employed for many years, working in furniture refinishing and design. It was very important to me to get a good night's rest the night before I made my deliveries as it took me about five to six hours to complete my runs. On one particular evening, when God had been telling me these very things, I went to sleep coming to God as a child totally trusting him to take care of me whether I got good rest or not. Simply said, I kind of had a "whatever happens" attitude. I confessed out loud, "God will give me the strength to do whatever I need to do." I kept my mind and thoughts focused on him and the promises in his Word. I recited scripture over and over in my mind till I drifted off to sleep. I ended up sleeping straight through the night for the first time in months without waking once, and the Lord even blessed me with more money than I had anticipated. Not only did God cause me to have such a sweet restful sleep, but he also rewarded me for heeding and being obedient to his Word. God is a rewarder for those who diligently seek him.

Hebrews 11:6 states, "But without faith, it is impossible to please and be satisfactory to him. For whoever would come near to God must [necessarily] believe that God exists and that he is the rewarder of those who earnestly [web: proceeding from an intense and serious state of mind] and diligently [web: steady, earnest and energetic application and effort, painstakingly] seek him out."

Yes, when we choose to obey his Word and do those things he instructs, he even rewards us. How awesome a God we serve!

WHO IS THE GREATEST IN THE KINGDOM OF HEAVEN?

At one point, during Jesus' reign here on earth, the disciples came and asked Jesus who was the greatest in the kingdom of heaven. We find the account in the book of Matthew.

Matthew 18:1–4 states, "At that time, the disciples came up and asked Jesus, who then is [really] the greatest in the kingdom of heaven?" (v. 1)

"He called a little child to himself and put him in the midst of them." (v. 2)

"And said, 'Truly I say to you, unless you repent [change, turn about] and become like this little child [trusting, lowly, web: free from self-assertive pride, loving, forgiving], you can never enter the kingdom of heaven [at all]." (v. 3)

God does not want us to have self-assertive pride about *anything* ever!

"Whoever will humble [web: not prideful, arrogant, or assertive, having a spirit of submission] himself therefore and become like this little child [trusting, lowly, free from self assertive pride, loving, forgiving] is greatest in the kingdom of heaven." (v. 4)

This is therefore contrary or opposite to what the world teaches, that the one who is the most self-assertive becomes the greatest and most successful. What a great revelation here God unfolds to us! If we really want to see the power of God unleashed in our lives, we can no longer be self-sufficient, but our sufficiency has to be from God.

2 Corinthians 3:5 states, "Not that we are fit [qualified and sufficient in ability] of ourselves to form personal judgments or to claim or count anything as coming from us, but our power and ability and sufficiency are from God."

GET A NEW MINDSET

There is freedom and liberty when we choose to change our thinking to what the Word says, instead of believing the same lies the devil has been tormenting our minds with for years.

2 Corinthians 3:17 states, "Now the Lord is the Spirit and where the spirit of the Lord is, there is liberty [emancipation from bondage, freedom]."

Emancipation, according to *Webster*, means "to free from restraint, control, or the power of another".

If we are not living by or under the control of God, then we are living under the power and control of the enemy. God wants us to be free from his control and influences. In order to do this, we have to get a new mindset. We must believe that with God, all things are possible. With man, some things may be impossible, but we serve a God who created everything we see out of nothing. Have you ever really thought about this? Take a moment to look around you, and look at all he has created. Even those things that are manmade, God has given the means, materials, intelligence, and ability to build those things. How truly amazing and of utmost intelligence he is! His means, possibilities, and resources are endless.

Jesus said in Luke 18:27, "But he said, 'What is impossible with men is possible with God.'"

Jeremiah also made this statement.

Jeremiah 32:17 states, "Alas, Lord God! You have made the heavens and the earth by your great power and by your outstretched arm! There is nothing too hard or too wonderful [web: marvelous, unusually good] for you."

Let God take your nothingness and watch him do a work in you. He has a plan for you that he wants to bring to fruition, but you must surrender all to him. We are the ones who limit him by our thinking. All he needs is your trust and obedience and *he will* do the rest!

Always remember, Jesus came to set *YOU* free. To tap into this freedom, we have to come to an end of our own abilities, saying, "Lord, I can't do this." But you can. Lean on, rely on, and trust in him for everything! He wants us to live by his strength and not ours and come to him as his child, letting him take care of us. Doesn't that just free your mind in doing just that? Let go and let God.

OUR STRENGTH AND STRONGHOLD

All over the Word, God tells us that he is our strength and stronghold. *Webster* defines strength as "capacity for exertion or endurance, tough, power of resisting attack". *Webster* defines stronghold as "a fortified place or a place of physical strength, courage and endurance; a place of security".

God desires that we know truth, that he is our strength and stronghold during adversity. The word *know* in the Greek is the word *ginosko*, which means to know something by experience. There is a difference between knowing something because you have been taught and knowing something by experience. God wants or desires for us all to know by experience.

I believe this is why he allows trials to come upon us, so we will experience for ourselves his hand and great power in hardships and battles that come upon us. Also, that we in turn tell others and give him the glory and praise.

A good example where the word *know* (ginosko) is used is found in the book of John where Jesus was speaking to the Jews.

John 8:31 and 32 states, "So Jesus said to those Jews who had believed in him, if you abide in my word [hold fast to my teachings and live in accordance with them], you are truly my disciples." (v. 31)

"And you will know [ginosko] the truth and the truth will set you free." (v. 32)

It isn't enough to just read the Word and say, "Oh, I know the Word." But we have to walk out in faith on the things God instructs to know his Word by experience, and that's what will set you free!

David knew by experience to seek God when he was faced with an attack of the enemy when he prayed to God while in distress in the book of Psalm. Let's read.

Psalm 64:1–3 states, "Hear my voice, O God, in my complaint; guard and preserve [web: to keep safe from injury, harm, or destruction] my life from the terror [web: one that inspires intense fear or a cause of anxiety] of the enemy." (v. 1)

David knew full well that intense fear and anxiety comes from our enemy, Satan, and prays to God to protect and keep him safe from his attacks.

"Hide [web: to conceal for shelter or protection] me from the secret counsel and conspiracy [web: the act of conspiring together] of the ungodly, from the scheming of evil doers." (v. 2)

Here, David asks God to keep him in the shelter of God from the secret plans of attack of the evil ones, the devil and all his followers. You see the enemy (the devil) carefully plans attacks against us in secret and until we come to the knowledge of the truth of God's Word, we don't even realize it is him behind them.

"Who whet [web: excite or stimulate] their tongues like a sword, who aim venomous [web: spiteful, malevolent, arising from an intense often vicious ill will, spite or hatred, criticism] words like arrows." (v. 3)

Remember, Satan hates us with a cruel hatred, and he is an accuser of the brethren.

Psalm 25:19 states, "Consider my enemies for they abound; they hate me with cruel hatred."

Revelation 12:10 states, "Then I heard a strong [loud] voice in heaven saying, Now it has come-the salvation and the power and the kingdom [the dominion, the reign] of our God and the power {the sovereignty, the authority] of his Christ [the Messiah]; for the accuser of our brethren, he who keeps bringing before our God charges against them day and night, has been cast out."

Satan is constantly going to God, pointing the finger at us so to speak, making his accusations. Example: "Oh, look what they're doing now, well if you allow me to do this to them, they certainly won't obey you then…" He is relentless! Now let's return to Psalm.

Psalm 64:4–10 states, "Who shoot from ambush [web: a trap which concealed persons lie in wait to attack by surprise] at the blameless man; suddenly do they shoot at him, without self-reproach [web: blaming oneself] or fear." (v. 4)

"They encourage themselves in an evil purpose, they talk of laying snares [web: something deceptively attractive; something by which one is entangled or involved in difficulties] secretly; they say, 'Who will discover us?'" (v. 5)

Are you getting this great revelation God is unfolding to you here, believer? When God had first opened up these scriptures to me, I was more than astounded! All I could think of was, "Oh, my gosh! Satan had been tricking me my whole life!" And I was completely unaware of all his ways until God unfolded these truths to me.

The enemy (Satan) has well laid out plans for your harm and will do anything to get you to take your focus off God and prompt you to do things contrary to or against what God says. We must be abreast and wise to look for these attacks, recognize where they are coming from, run to Jesus our Savior, and do those things he instructs. The devil thinks you will never suspect he is behind these schemes.

"They think out acts of injustice and say, We have indeed accomplished a well devised thing! For the inward thought of each one [talking about us, humans] [is unsearchable] and his heart is deep." (v. 6)

To get a deeper understanding of this verse, let's re-read the same verse in the New International Version.

Psalm 64:6 states, "They plot injustice and say, We have devised a perfect plan! Surely the human mind and heart are cunning [web: characterized by wiliness and trickery, prettily appealing]." (NIV)

The devil is very well aware that in our flesh dwells no good thing and therefore preys upon our flesh, knowing how easily tricked we are. He thinks his plans against us are perfect.

But if we are praying to God and are keeping our focus on him, drawing forth wisdom from his Word, trusting him in these attacks, then God shows us what he will do to our enemy.

"But God will shoot an unexpected arrow at them; and suddenly, they shall be wounded." (v. 7)

Here, after David prays to the Lord to help him against the devil or Satan, God overturns the attacks, helps him, and promises to do the same for us if we draw our strength from and take refuge in him.

"And they will be made to stumble [web: fall or move carelessly] their own tongues turning against them; all who gaze upon them will shake their heads and flee away." (v. 8)

God will cause the enemies plans to fail, and they will flee away!

I wanted to note here once again as I've mentioned previously, that the enemy will try to work through people around you as well to get you to stumble or become distressed. Many of whom are unaware that they are being used by him as his little puppets sotospeak. He is ultimately out to steal, kill, and destroy them as well. So we must not put blame on them either but rather love them as God instructs for their eyes are blinded to the truth. That's why when Jesus was being crucified, he prayed to the Father and said, "Father, forgive them, for they know not what they do." (Luke 23:34a)

"And all men shall [reverently] fear and be in awe [web: profound and humbly fearful reverence, inspired by something sacred or mysterious], and they will declare the work of God for they will wisely consider and acknowledge that it is his doing." (v. 9)

Here is the knowledge by experience where the people will see that the deliverance from the enemy is indeed by the hand of our God!

"The [uncompromisingly] righteous shall be glad in the Lord and shall trust and take refuge in him; and all the upright in heart shall glory and offer praise [to God!]." (v. 10)

What a great revelation God gives us here through his Word. He warns us that we have an enemy (Satan), and he will be attacking us day and night; he never sleeps. He (God) knows our own strength will fail us as we cannot fight the spiritual within our flesh and that we need to come to him to be our strength and stronghold!

Psalm 18:2 and 3 states, "The Lord is my rock, my fortress [web: a place of security and strength] and my Deliverer, my God, my keen and firm strength in whom I will trust and take refuge [web: shelter or protection from danger or distress], my shield and my horn of my salvation, my high tower." (v. 2)

"I will call upon the Lord who is to be praised; so shall I be saved from my enemies." (v. 3)

What do you do when you are in trouble or wrapped in difficulties? *CALL UPON THE LORD*

Psalm 27:1 and 2 states, "The Lord is my Light and my Salvation, whom shall I fear or dread? The Lord is the Refuge and Stronghold of my Life, of whom shall I be afraid?" (v. 1)

"When the wicked, even my enemies and my foes came upon me to eat up my flesh, they stumbled and fell." (v. 2)

God absolutely instructs us *NOT* to rely on our own fleshly human strength, but to rely and lean upon *HIM* in all things.

Jeremiah 17:5 states, "Thus says the Lord: Cursed [with great evil] is the strong man who trusts in and relies on frail man, making weak [human] flesh his arm and whose mind and heart turn aside from the Lord."

We need to keep our stay and focus upon him till the calamities and storms are over and not trusting in our weak and frail human flesh.

Psalm 57:1 states, "Be merciful and gracious to me O God, be merciful and gracious to me for my soul takes refuge and finds shelter and confidence in you; yes in the shadow of your wings will I take refuge and be confident until calamities [web: a state of deep distress or misery] and destructive storms [web: to attack, take or win over by storm] are passed."

When Satan was attacking my mind and body through panic and anxiety, the Lord gave me two verses of scripture that I quickly wrote down on my index cards. I can't express to you enough how they helped me when all hell was coming against me. I still continue to read and meditate upon verses even to this day. May I suggest that you do the same.

The first one is found in the book of Isaiah.

Isaiah 41:10 states, "Fear not, there is nothing to fear for I am with you, do not look around you in terror [web: state of intense fear, worry or anxiety] and be dismayed [web: deprived of courage through the pressure of sudden fear, anxiety, or great perplexity, state of being full of difficulty] for I am your God. I will strengthen [web: to make stronger in the power of resisting attack] and harden [web: not easily yielding to pressure, to be confirmed or strengthened in opposition] you to difficulties, yes, I will help you, yes. I will hold you up and retain [web: to hold secure or intact] you with my [victorious] right hand of rightness and justice."

God commands us here to *FEAR NOT*! He says there is nothing to fear because he is with you. Notice how he says "do not look around you in terror". He wants us to always look to him, not at the terror the enemy is presenting. Then, he mentions twice that he promises to give us strength and help in difficulties. (When something is mentioned twice, it is twice established and is of utmost importance).

The second verse is also in the book of Isaiah.

Isaiah 41:13 states, "For I the Lord your God hold your right hand; I am the Lord who says to you, Fear not; I will help [web: give assistance or support, rescue, save oneself out of a difficulty] you!"

After reading these verses, whenever I was being attacked through fear and panic, I would go and do the things I needed to do despite how I felt and would picture God in my mind, holding my hand as I pressed through. This really helped me countless times during my trials. I would even say, "Okay, Lord, it's you and me, and I trust you will bring me through, and I will put your promise to the test." He never let me down, no, not even once and gave me the strength and help just as he promised he would! In fact, all fear and anxieties fled as I kept moving forward with him. Breakthroughs most often come not before but as you press through circumstances!
God backs up every promise in his Word and wants us to lean upon those promises in times of trouble.

Isaiah 55:11 states, "So shall my Word be that goes forth out of My mouth; it shall not return to Me void [without producing any effect, useless] but it shall accomplish that which I please and purpose, and it shall prosper in the thing for which I sent it."

The devil or Satan always wants to make God out to be a liar. Remember when he told Eve, "did God really say, you shall not eat of every tree of the garden?" (Genesis 3:1) And also, when he made the statement to her, "You shall not surely die." (Genesis 3:4) This was after God had already told Adam and Eve that they would surely die!

We need to stop listening to the lies he whispers in our ears and hold fast to the truth of God's Word; he never lies!

Numbers 23:19 states, "God is not a man that he should tell or act a lie neither the son of man that he should feel repentance or compunction [web: distress of mind over an anticipated action] for what he has promised. Has he said and shall he not do it? Or has he spoken and shall he not make it good?"

God is telling us here that he never lies, therefore we can rely on him always. God says what he means and means what he says!

ISAIAH RECALLS GOD'S PROMISES

Isaiah 25:1, 4 and 8 states, "Oh Lord, you are my God; I will exalt you, I will praise your name, for you have done wonderful things, even purposes planned of old [and fulfilled] in faithfulness and truth." (v. 1)

Here, Isaiah is recalling how God honored and backed up his promises in fulfilling his plans, just like he said he would in times past.

"For you have been a stronghold [web: a place of security or survival] for the poor, a stronghold for the needy in distress [web: subject to great strain or difficulties] a shelter [web: state of being covered and protected] from the storm [web: a violent assault on a defended position], a shade [web: to shelter or screen by intercepting heat] from the heat [web: the height or stress of an action or condition; example: in the heat of battle] for the blast of the ruthless ones [or attacks from our enemy, Satan] is like a rainstorm against a wall." (v. 4)

God is telling us here that he puts up a wall (figuratively speaking) against our enemies attacks when we follow and trust him.

"He will swallow up death [in victory; he will abolish death forever]. And the Lord God will wipe away tears from all faces; And the reproach [web: a cause or occasion of blame, discredit, or disgrace] of His people He will take away from all the earth; for the Lord has spoken it." (v. 8)

Satan, our enemy, loves to accuse, discredit, and bring disgrace upon us, but one day, he will be destroyed. But for now, we are instructed to shut him out and not buy into his lies.

HEEDING GOD'S VOICE

God wants us all to pay close attention to his voice and the words of truth. He wants us to know by experience the truths that he sets forth in his Holy Word (the Bible). In other words to walk in that truth!

Isaiah 30:20 and 21 states, "And though the Lord gives you the bread of adversity and the water of affliction, yet your Teacher will not hide Himself anymore, but your eyes will constantly behold your Teacher." (v. 20)

God is our Teacher!

"And your ears will hear a word behind you saying, 'This is the way, walk in it, when you turn to the right hand and when you turn to the left.'" (v. 21)

How do we learn to walk in this way of truth? By following his instructions to us by reading and studying his Word and obeying what we read!

1 Timothy 4:13states, "Till I come, devote yourself to [public and private] reading, to exhortation [preaching and personal appeals] and to teaching and instilling doctrine."

God is instructing us to read and study his Word, teaching others as well until the Lord returns.

Deuteronomy 28:1 and 2 states, "If you will listen diligently [web: steady, earnest, and energetic application and effort] to the voice of the Lord Your God, being watchful to do all his commandments which I command you this day, the Lord your God will set you high above all the nations of the earth." (v. 1)

"And all these blessings shall come upon you and overtake [web: to come upon suddenly] you if you heed [web: pay attention to] the voice of the Lord your God." (v. 2)

I would like you to re-read these two verses again. Through these scriptures, God is trying to reveal a very important message and promise to us. He says, Listen to his voice, not the voice of what the world is telling you or the negative voice of the enemy. Listen to God's voice (what he speaks to you through his Word), and after you've heard his voice, you need to put it into application in your life, doing those things he instructs. You do this by changing your mind to think the Word, regardless of circumstances and then act upon that Word. Then, the Lord tells us here that, if you do this, blessings shall come upon you suddenly! You can't just do this for a fleeting moment here and there and expect results. You need to be consistent. As God states in verse 1, we have to listen to God's voice diligently or with a steady application, and then we shall reap the blessing or desired result.

I personally have experienced this very thing over and over during some heavy waves of attacks from our enemy. My whole being was filled with anxiety and panic, just wanting to fly away or stay in my house and pull the covers over my head. Then, after readying and studying the Word, shutting out all negatives around me, diligently listening to God's voice, *suddenly*, I am restored to a peaceful state of mind and being—the state by which God desires for us all to have constantly. If we would only make his Word of utmost importance in our daily lives and do those things that he instructs, then we shall experience the more than abundant life that he called us out to live!

GOD PROMISES BLESSINGS

Webster's definition of the word *blessed* is "to enjoy the bliss of heaven, bringing pleasure or contentment". If we make up our minds to follow God and his Word, God promises we shall be blessed. Let's look again in the book of Deuteronomy.

Deuteronomy 28:3 and 4 states, "Blessed shall you be in the city [the place where you live] and blessed shall you be in the field [the place where you work]." (v. 3)

"Blessed shall be the fruit of your body [your health] and the fruit of your ground [your endeavors] and the fruit of your beasts, the increase of your cattle and the young of your flock." (v. 4)

Deuteronomy 28:8, 13 and 14 states, "The Lord shall command the blessing upon you in your store house and all that you undertake. And he will bless you in the land which the Lord your God gives you." (v. 8)

Every blessing that you have in your life comes from God.

"And the Lord shall make you the head and not the tail; and you shall be above only and you shall not be beneath; if you heed the commandments of the Lord your God which I command you this day and are watchful to do them." (v. 13)

All these blessings is promised to us upon a condition, that we diligently (web: steady and energetic application and effort) harken or listen to the voice of our God and do those things he instructs through his Word. God, in turn, promises to prosper or take care of all our concerns in all relations of our lives both external and internal.

"And you shall not turn aside from any of the words which I command you this day to the right hand or to the left to go after other gods to serve them." (v. 14)

Going after other gods simply means the following: Buddah, god of the sun, moon, or stars or any other gods, except the one true God (the author of the bible) who inspired true followers to record scripture as God inspired them to do so (moved by the Holy Spirit).

Many believers do not realize that anything we put before God becomes a god to us. It could be our jobs, sports, TV, relationships, or even family. God desires that he be above and first and foremost in our lives; therefore, seek him first always. Everything else should be secondary to him.

2 Timothy 3:15–17 states, "And how from your childhood you have had a knowledge of and been acquainted with the sacred Writings, which are able to instruct you and give you the understanding for salvation which comes through faith in Christ Jesus [through the leaning of the entire human personality on God in Christ Jesus in absolute trust and confidence in His power, wisdom and goodness]. (v. 15)

"Every Scripture is God-breathed [given by his inspiration] and profitable for instruction, for reproof and conviction of sin, for correction of error and discipline in obedience, [and] for training in righteousness [in holy living, in conformity to God's will in thought, purpose, and action]." (v. 16)

Notice here how Gods says "for instruction and correction of error". Until we come to know the truth of God's Word, we are living our lives in error and need his instruction to live correctly.

"So that the man of God may be complete [web: to make whole] and proficient [web: well advanced in a branch of knowledge], well fitted and thoroughly equipped for every good work." (v. 17)

God so desires that we be made whole and have a thorough knowledge of him and his Word, so that we can live for the purposes in which he called us out to live.

2 Peter 1:21 states, "For no prophecy ever originated because some man willed it [to do so, it never came by human impulse], but men spoke from God who were borne along [moved and impelled] by the Holy Spirit."

So you see here that man did not just decide to write the Bible. God moved in these men and women to record the scriptures because God wanted us to know the truth to obtain the life that he had planned for us from the beginning. Living in fear and panic was not part of his plan, but he knew we would be attacked by it and thus addresses it over and over in His Word.

HOW TO RESPOND DURING TRIALS

Even though God gives us his promise of blessings if we heed his voice and do those things he instructs, it doesn't mean we are exempted from going through trials and tribulations while here on earth. Jesus told us we would endure trials in the book of John.

John 16:33 states, "I have told you these things, so that in Me you may have [perfect] peace and confidence. In the world, you will have tribulation and trials and distress and frustration; but be of good cheer [take courage; be confident, certain, undaunted; web: fearless in the face of stress]! For I have overcome the world. [I have deprived it of power to harm you and have conquered it for you]."

Jesus already conquered our enemy the devil and has already given us the power through the Holy Spirit. We need to learn how to unleash that power in our lives! God indeed shows us how and gives us wisdom on how to overcome the attacks of the enemy each and every time if we just keep our focus on him not looking to the left or the right, seeking wisdom through his Word.

In the book of Proverbs, we find God had given Solomon skillful and godly wisdom. Solomon tells us how we are to walk in this life.

Proverbs 4:25–27 states, "Let your eyes look right on [with fixed purpose] and let your gaze be straight before you." (v. 25)

To let your eyes look right on with fixed purpose is by not letting anything hinder you, letting your gaze be straight before you, with your eyes and thoughts fixed on God's Word.

"Consider [web: to think about with care or caution] well the path of your feet and let all your ways be established [web: set on a firm basis] and ordered aright [web: correctly]." (v. 26)

How many of us go through life not even thinking about where it could lead us or even where we're going? God wants us to really think about with care and caution where we are going and what we are doing. He wants all our ways to be set on the firm basis of the Word correctly.

"Turn not aside to the right hand or the left; remove your foot from evil [web: something that brings sorrow, distress, or calamity; an extraordinary grave event marked by great loss and lasting distress and persistent suffering and trouble]." (v. 27)

God does not want us to focus or give attention to what the enemy is presenting to your mind and body.

God explained this to me in this way, to have tunnel vision, so to speak

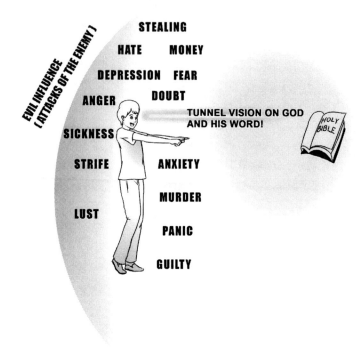

In other words, don't look or put your focus on the evil the enemy is trying to attack you with but keep your eyes and focus upon God and his Word at all times (even confessing it aloud during your trial or attack). When we do this, we unleash the power of God to overcome these attacks and see God fighting back for us! I can't express enough how very important this is to do. It is *KEY* to your success! It has a mathematical exactness!

Just as 1+1=2, so does Attacks from the enemy + God's wisdom = Victory!

GOD FIGHTS FOR US!

Deuteronomy 20:3 and 4 states, "And you shall say to them, Hear O Israel, you draw near this day to battle against your enemies. Let not your [minds and] hearts faint [web: lose courage]; fear not and do not tremble or be terrified [and in dread] because of them."

When writing this particular verse on my index card, I felt the Lord urge me on to replace the "O Israel" and insert my name here, making it more personal to me. Example: Hear, O Grace, you draw near this day to battle against your enemies (speaking ultimately of Satan and all his hosts). Let not your mind and heart lose courage; fear not and do not tremble or be terrified and in dread because of them.

How many times when the enemy attacks you with fear and panic, do you start to feel this overwhelming sense of dread, where you don't feel like moving forward to do something? Where you actually feeling immobilized? Well, know for a surety, believer, that this is an attack coming straight from the pit of hell. The devil will try to trick your mind into thinking that you cannot move forward, but God says in this battle to *NOT* let your mind and heart lose courage. Then, he says fear not, don't be afraid of this and do not tremble (web: shake or quiver) or be terrified (web: deterred or intimidated) and in dread. *Webster's* meaning of the word *dread* is "to feel extreme reluctance to meet or face; to be apprehensive or fearful". The devil is very crafty and cunning, and his attacks can seem so real, shaking us to our core if we allow them. I can remember being taught early on in my teachings that *FEAR* is False Evidence Appearing Real! The devil can make things to appear so real to us by attacking our minds so severely that it manifests over into our bodies and then our actions. That's why he does it! We have to recognize this right at the onset of the attack. Keep moving forward with God, regardless of the attack, and God promises to save or deliver us as found in the next verse of Deuteronomy 20.

"For the Lord your God is He who goes with you to fight [web: attempt to prevent the success or effectiveness] for you against your enemies to save [web: rescue or deliver from danger or harm; prevent an opponent from winning] you." (v. 4)

Notice here how it says, "For the Lord your God is he who goes with you." This denotes action on our part. How can God go with us if we don't move forward in the midst of an attack of fear? As I've stated previously, this is key to your success! Keep moving forward with God and watch him deliver you from the enemies grip.

During my study and writing of this book, I went to a routine check up to have a mammogram done. The mammogram was performed and, like most women, I didn't really give that much thought to it. After about ten days, I received a call from my doctor. She stated that there seemed to be something that didn't look quite normal and wanted me to follow up with an ultrasound. Still, with little care or concern, I proceeded to have that done as she suggested. During the ultrasound procedure, I calmly asked the technician, "Is everything okay?" She began to point out on the screen a questionable mass in the area of concern. Of course, this now got my attention and I asked, "Is this something that looks dangerous or cancerous according to your professional experience?" She quickly responded with, "The doctor will be in soon to discuss this with you." Almost immediately, the fear and panic overwhelmed me! "God, what is going on, I asked?" As thoughts of surgical removal of my breast, death, and all sorts of negatives flooded my mind, the doctor finally came in. She then explained to me that it wasn't normal and raised suspicion. She wanted me to have the area biopsied. I can remember this blank look on both the doctor and technicians faces which scared me even more. I left shortly after, tears flowing down my face as they escorted me out the back door. I even thought it strange that they took me out the back door instead of where I had originally came in.

I just couldn't believe what was going on. *Why me,* I thought. I asked the Lord, "Now what?" He replied, "Are you going to trust me?" After feeling sorry for myself, I finally said, "Yes, Lord, even in this too, I will trust you!"

Weeks had passed before my biopsy appointment, and every time, Satan tried to attack my mind with the negative thoughts of doubt, worry, fear, and panic, I kept my focus on God with my mind stayed on the promises of the Word. I kept repeating aloud, "Lord, I trust you, this battle is yours to fight, not mine."

The day finally arrived to have the biopsy performed. I flooded my heart and mind with the truth of his Word as he instructs us to do.

Ephesians 6:14a states, "Stand therefore [hold your ground], having tightened the belt of truth around your loins."

I had my normal fellowship with the Lord first thing that morning. The procedure was to be done while I was awake, and I told God that I wanted him to give me a scripture that I could write down on one of my index cards to read over and over during the procedure. He gave me two that morning.

Psalm 27:14 states, "Wait and hope for and expect the Lord; be brave and of good courage and let your heart be stout [web: brave and bold] and enduring [web: to remain firm under suffering or misfortune without yielding; undergo a hardship without giving in]."

Isaiah 41:13 states, "For I the Lord your God, hold your right hand; I am the Lord who says to you, Fear not: I will help you!"

During the drive down to the appointment, my heart and mind were at total peace, trusting in him. He gave me the confidence and comfort I needed.

As the technician began to prep me for the surgery, I could feel my body start to tremble a bit (Satan still trying to attack me) as she explained to me the procedure. While lying there, I held up my index card above my head, so I could read the two scriptures God had given. I kept reading it over and over to keep God in my main focus and his Word in the forefront of my mind. *Okay, Lord, let's get this over with,* I thought.

The doctor finally came in to perform the biopsy. She looked over at me and saw the index card with my scriptures and asked, "What is that you're reading?" I told her they were scriptures from the Bible and said, "I don't do anything without my Lord!" She began to comment that she was a spiritual person herself. I felt somewhat relieved and asked her if she was a Christian too. She answered back and said, "No, I'm Muslim." *Okay, God, your hands behind hers,* I thought. And at that point, I looked up toward the ceiling and saw an image of Jesus looking back down at me. I knew I wasn't alone!

She began to probe around to pinpoint the area to be biopsied and to all of our amazement, she couldn't find it. She then had the technician go back to the previous ultrasound screens to where they first saw the images of the mass. "Here it is," said the technician as she pointed it out. Still probing around, the doctor kept saying, "I see it on the previous screens, but I can't find it now!"

"I don't see it, it's not there, everything seems to be normal." She said over and over. She then looked over at me and said, "You must have been praying really hard!" I told her that God can do anything! I then asked her if this means that I don't have to have the procedure done and she replied, "There's nothing here for me to biopsy." She then put the probe down and asked, "What's on those cards anyway? I want to write it down." I told her what the scriptures were as my heart leaped for joy! What a witness to see the power of God fulfill his promise when we do those things he instructs. Not only was this a testimony to me, but to the technician and doctor as well.

Tears of joy started to stream down my face in praise and thankfulness as I left there that day, only this time with Jesus escorting me out the door!

Chapter
11

God Promises to Deliver

HAVE PATIENCE

We live in such a world where we want everything right now. The computers aren't running fast enough, people are driving too slow, food not served quickly enough, and the list goes on and on.

In fact, patience was never a long suit of mine. If things didn't happen for me right away, I would tend to get anxious and frustrated, sometimes even angry. Even in my job, though I was very efficient, I was always rushing to get orders out, bringing me a lot of stress and strain. We live in such a fast-paced society that it dictates anything but patience.

I can remember one day, the Lord spoke to my heart and said, "Why are you always rushing? No one ever said everything you do has to be done in a hurry. *SLOW DOWN!*"

Thinking about what the Lord had said, I thought to myself, I don't know why I rush or why I wanted to have everything right away.

Even through my trials of fear and panic, I wanted deliverance right away. I would say things to the Lord like, "Father, I know you can deliver me right now." Then, only to be frustrated that I wasn't. Yes, God can deliver right away, but sometimes, he doesn't because he wants to teach us something. I know for a fact, that had he delivered me right away, I wouldn't have experienced what many people are going through—suffering in this area of fear and panic to the extent that I was, which lead me to the writing of this book.

Even though these trials came upon me, God had been there giving me the strength and courage I needed to endure each and every time. I still did not feel completely set free. I would ask God, why? "Why can't you just take this from me right now?" And he replied, "I am leading you the long hard way, so you will learn to lean on me constantly and for everything. I have a plan for you. I will see you through! Quit being a coward and quit thinking *what if?* Lean on me and me alone!"

The Lord is spirit and where the spirit is, there is freedom. As we continue in the Word, we are delivered and transfigured little by little, every day.

2 Corinthians 3:17 and 18 states, "Now the Lord is the Spirit, and where the Spirit of the Lord is, there is liberty [emancipation from bondage, freedom]." (v. 17)

"And all of us, as with unveiled face, [because we] continued to behold [web: to gaze upon, observe] in the Word of God as in a mirror the glory of the Lord, are constantly being transfigured [web: transformed outwardly for the better] into His very own image in ever increasing splendor and from one degree of glory to another; [for this comes] from the Lord [Who is Spirit]." (v. 18)

This is how the Lord explained it to me.

Just as people do physical workouts to exercise their bodies to get fit, we need to exercise our minds in order to get to a way of right thinking. Start to practice 'tunnel vision on God's Word, blocking out all negatives around you and keeping your focus on God and his Word every day. Each time you do this, it will become easier and eventually become automatic. Just as it was automatic for you to think about the negatives Satan has been presenting, it will become automatic for you to think the Word. But always remember, believer, we have to be constantly feeding ourselves with the Word of God. Until we get to that point in our lives, God allows obstacles so that we will learn to lean on him and seek his Word for our strength and help in all humbleness, not becoming prideful.

Wow! This was truly a great revelation he gave me that day! It reminded me of Paul in the book of Corinthians.

PAUL'S THORN IN THE FLESH

Note: I know I mentioned this previously, but the Lord prompted me to go over this again to you. Obviously, something he wanted to establish twice: Paul complained of a thorn in his flesh and asked God to remove it. We find the account in 2 Corinthians.

2 Corinthians 12:7–10 states, "And to keep me from being puffed up and too much elated [web: prideful] by the exceeding greatness of these revelations, there was given me a thorn [web: something that causes stress or irritation] in the flesh, a messenger of Satan, to rack [web: cause to suffer torture, pain, or anguish] and buffet [web: strike repeatedly] and harass [web: exhaust, fatigue, to annoy persistently] me; to keep me from being excessively exalted." (v. 7)

Let's first look at the attacks Paul suffered and how he recognized where or by whom the attacks came when he stated, "a messenger of Satan." Paul knew full well that he was in a spiritual battle and that his enemy was indeed Satan. Second thing he mentions here is that God allowed this because he didn't want Paul to become prideful. You see, as you begin to really start seeking God and begin deeply studying his Word, God opens up your eyes to a whole new world of knowledge, that you will start to see things that others do not. It is out of the humanness of our flesh and the sin that lies within us all to get tempted with pride. This is how Satan fell, through pride. He thought he was better than God! God does not ever want to see us prideful but receive his Word with all humbleness, giving him the glory and praise always. Paul didn't ask once but three times for God to remove this thorn until God answered him in the next verse.

"Three times, I called upon the Lord and besought [web: ask in a serious and emotional way to do something] him about this and begged that it might depart from me." (v. 8)

Obviously, Paul was extremely bothered by this attack on his flesh. No one knows exactly what it was, and the Bible does not clearly state what it was. I've often wondered if it was this attack of fear and panic. Then, God answers Paul.

"But he said to me, my grace [my favor, loving kindness, and mercy] is enough for you [sufficient against any danger and enables you to bear; [web: put up with by being supported (by God) the trouble manfully]; for my strength and power are made perfect [fulfilled and completed] in your weakness. Therefore, I will all the more gladly glory [web: rejoice proudly in God's physical strength] in my weaknesses and infirmities [web: weakness of mind, will, or character] that the strength and power of Christ [the Messiah] may rest upon me!" (v. 9)

God does not want us to depend on our fleshly human abilities or our own strengths. We are all in a spiritual battle and need God's divine strength to deliver us. Because of his great love, favor, and mercy upon us, he promises to help us always!

"So for the sake of Christ, I am well pleased and take pleasure in infirmities, insults, hardships, persecutions, perplexities [web: filled with uncertainties or difficulties] and distresses; for when I am weak [in human strength], then am I [truly] strong [able, powerful in divine strength]." (v. 10)

Don't you too want to get to this point in your spiritual walk with God as Paul did? Where you actually take pleasure in the trials or attacks of the enemy because you know by experience that God will bring you out victoriously each and every time? And that you will see his mighty working power and ability in your life! This is where you will find the more than abundant life that Jesus died for, and God promises to give to those of us who believe. You will *NEVER* find it unless you walk in the truth of God's Holy Word!

GOD DESIRES FOR US TO KNOW TRUTH

Without truth (God's Holy Word), we will never live this life with the freedom, love, and joy that God intended for us all to have. Like I've stated previously, we need not read just five or ten minutes here and there; although of course, this does profit little but certainly not to live the life God called us out to live, enjoying the bliss of freedom. We need to study his Word as Paul writes in the book of Timothy.

2 Timothy 2:15, 25 and 26 states, "Study [web: read in detail with the intent of learning] and be eager [web: enthusiastic] and do your utmost to present yourself to God approved [tested by trial] a workman who has no cause to be ashamed, correctly analyzing and accurately dividing the Word of Truth." (v. 15)

If you want God to unfold the many truths in his Word and live that more than abundant life he has planned for you, then you need to do as he instructs us here and that is to study.

"He must correct his opponents with courtesy and gentleness in the hope that God may grant that they will repent and come to know the Truth [that they will perceive and recognize and become accurately acquainted with and acknowledge it]." (v. 25)

God desires we all know truth! Why? God tells us in the next verse.

"And that they may come to their senses [and] escape out of the snare [web: trap, something by which one is entangled, involved in difficulties, something deceptively attractive] of the devil, having been held captive by him, [henceforth] to do His [God's] will." (v. 26)

Here, God unfolds to us why he wants us to know the truth of his Word when he says he wants us to come to our senses or be in right frame of mind or to think correctly. Also, that we may escape out of the snare or traps of the devil. When we do not know or understand truth, we can become easily tricked by the devil and actually be held captive by him without even knowing it, hindering us to do God's will. You don't have to be possessed by the devil to be held captive by him; therefore, I am not speaking of devil possession. He can and will hold you captive in your mind through your thought process if you don't know and walk in the truth, which produces right thinking and freedom. Thinking right thoughts is thinking the truth of God's Word instead of the negative thoughts and lies Satan tries to present to your mind. Let me explain it in this way. Since the day you were born, you have been taught many things as you went on your way through life. Your mind has been open to accept any and all things in your thought process, whether positive or negative, good or evil. Your mind has been an open door, so to speak. Satan is very well aware of this fact as well and therefore starts to prey upon us at a very young age, bombarding us with all kinds of negative thoughts. Some of which are the following: fear, doubt, worry, condemnation, anxiety, depression, lying, stealing, murder, lust, etc. The list goes on and on. We live our lives, entertaining these negative thoughts and unknowingly suspecting that it is him (Satan) because of our ignorance and not knowing the truth of God's Word. This is what the Bible speaks of when it says, "their eyes were blinded." After you read and study the Word, God opens your eyes to see truth. Until then, if we go on dwelling on those negative thoughts, we create habit patterns in our thought process. After years of doing this, they eventually become a normal way of thinking for us. This is what builds strongholds in our minds built by the devil himself after infiltrating our minds for years with all kinds of negative and evil thoughts, which all lead to our own destruction. Remember, the devil's plan as was from the beginning is to steal, kill, and destroy us all because he hates God and all he has created!

You can *never* win with the devil! He will use you if you allow him. He will even be good to you for a season, but his ultimate plan in the end for you is destruction. Don't be fooled by him! Jesus warned us of the devil's plans but also tells us of his plans to bless if we adhere to him and his ways.

John 10:10 states, "The thief comes only in order to steal, kill and destroy, I came that they may have and enjoy life and have it in abundance [to the fullest, till it overflows]."

Let's look at the word *thief* in this verse. In Greek, it is the word, *kleptes*, which means robber. In the Strongs Concordance, the word, *kleptes*, means a thief who steals by stealth (in secret) rather than in the open with violence. In the Thayers Greek Lexicon, *kleptes* means embezzler or name for false teachers who do not care to instruct men but abuse their confidence for their own gain.

The devil is a robber who wants to steal our freedom and abundant life in Christ. He does this in secret, thinking we will never suspect that it is him!

Jesus on the other hand, came so that we may have and enjoy life, a life flowing in abundance! We have to make a choice, and there are only two choices or options that we have:

Either we will believe Satan and his lies, dwelling on the negatives that he presents to our minds that lead to destruction or...

Believe God and the truth he gives us through his Word, dwelling on the positives therein that will lead to freedom and life everlasting.

That's it! We have to choose.

DESTRUCTION OF STRONGHOLDS

Let us first look at the word, *stronghold*. In Greek, the word, *stronghold*, is *ochuroma* which means "fortress or fortified place". Now that we know the devil has been building his strongholds in our minds after years of infiltrating our thoughts with all kinds of negative and evil thoughts, how do we begin to be set free from these strongholds, allowing God's Word to become a stronghold in our minds? We need to go to the book of Corinthians, where I previously stated about our spiritual weapons.

2 Corinthians 10:3–5 states, "For though we walk [live] in the flesh, we are not carrying on our warfare according to the flesh and using mere human weapons." (v. 3)

"For the weapons of our warfare are not physical [weapons of flesh and blood] but they are mighty before God for the over-throw and destruction of strongholds." (v. 4)

God is fully aware of these strongholds set up by Satan to cloud our thinking and explains how to overthrow or destroy them in the next verse.

"(Inasmuch as we) Refute [web: show to be false] arguments and theories and reasonings and every proud and lofty [web: having a haughty or prideful overbearing manner] thing that sets itself up against the [true] knowledge of God and we lead every thought and purpose away captive into the obedience of Christ [the Messiah, the Anointed One]." (v. 5)

For even better clarity, let's re-read this same verse in the King James Version.

2 Corinthians 10:5 states, "Casting down imaginations [web: the act or power of forming a mental image of something not present to the senses or never before wholly perceived in reality] and every high thing that exalteth itself against the knowledge of God and bring into captivity every thought to the obedience of Christ." (KJV)

So to break free from the strongholds by which our enemy, Satan, has kept you bound is to show to be false any arguments or theories, reasoning, or prideful things that is contrary to what God tells you in his Word. Then, God says to lead *EVERY* thought captive (web: kept within bounds, held under control) to the obedience of Christ. The obedience of Christ is to think and be obedient to God's Word constantly. In other words, you're in a situation and you feel fear, doubt, panic, or anxiety, etc. arising in your thoughts which you've experienced before due to the stronghold the devil has built in your mind. Now, to combat these negative thoughts, you replace these thoughts with God's Word. This is spiritual warfare! It may be replacing that thought with something like "I can do all things through Christ which strengtheneth me." (Philippians 4:13, KJV) The point is to replace *every thought* that does not line up with God's Word to God's Word! Every negative thought that is contrary to God's Word is an assault of evil, whether through thought or even feelings. Have you ever thought the following? "Well, I feel afraid, depressed, worried, but I don't know why." "I have no reason to feel this way." Or perhaps even circumstances around you aren't going your way, causing you to feel the way you do. Well, know, believer, you are under attack! Remember, Satan can and will set up schemes to affect people around you and circumstances to try to get us to take our focus off our God and his Word, to steal our peace, joy, and love.

God tells us in the book of Timothy that *HE WILL* deliver us from every assault of evil.

2 Timothy 4:18 states, "[And indeed] The Lord will certainly deliver and draw me to himself from every assault [web: a violent physical or verbal attack] of evil. He will preserve and bring me safe unto His Heavenly Kingdom. To [him] be the glory forever and ever. [Amen]."

Yes, Satan can and will attack you physically and verbally. How do we know? Because God says it here and warns us against it.

FIRM INSTRUCTION AGAINST SATAN

God would never tell us that we have an enemy (Satan) that would be attacking us day and night and not give us instruction, leaving us helpless. We are all vulnerable to his attacks, but God gives us power to overcome his attacks. He (God) addresses and shows us how in his Word. Let us look now at the instruction he gives.

1 Peter 5:7 states, "Casting the whole of your care [all your anxieties, all your worries, all your concerns, once and for all] on Him, for he cares for you affectionately and cares about you watchfully [web: no sleep or rest, carefully observant]."

Wow! God instructs us here to give Him ALL things that bother us and that he doesn't take his eyes off us for a second (he never sleeps), always looking out for us.

Psalm 55:22 states, "Cast your burden on the Lord [releasing the weight of it] and he will sustain [web: give support or relief to] you: He will never allow the righteous to be moved [made to slip, fall, or fail]!"

What a promise God gives us here! God instructs us to cast, get rid of, or discard all our burdens unto him and not dwell on them or keep them in our minds and hearts.

1 Peter 5:8–10 states, "Be well balanced [temperate, sober of mind], be vigilant [web: alertly watchful to avoid danger] and cautious at all times, for that enemy of yours, the devil roams around like a lion roaring [in fierce hunger] seeking someone to seize upon and devour." (v. 8)

Here, God specifically warns us to be carefully watching out for the devil because he roams around in this world, just waiting to pounce on anyone willing to take his bait and buying into his lies.

"Withstand [web: oppose with firm determination, resist successfully] him, be firm in faith [against his onset-rooted, established, strong, immovable, and determined] knowing that the same [identical] sufferings are appointed to your brotherhood [the whole body of Christians] throughout the world." (v. 9)

God tells us to be firm, rooted, and grounded (in his Word and in faith, believing) at the devil's onset or at the very beginning of his attacks.

"And after you have suffered a little while, the God of all Grace [who imparts all blessing and favor] Who has called you to his [own] eternal glory in Christ Jesus, will Himself complete and make you what you ought to be, establish and ground you securely and strengthen and settle you." (v. 10)

Here, God tells us that we may suffer a little while, *but* when we keep doing those things he is instructing us (which is being firm on the promises of his Word), he will ground us securely, give us strength, and settle us. Instead of getting discouraged or giving up in prayer or studying the Word (which is exactly what Satan wants you to do), we need to persevere under trial and keep moving forward with God. We need to put one foot in front of the other, not looking to the left or right at the negatives Satan is attacking us with, whether physical or verbal, but keeping our focus on God and what his Word says. Don't be surprised at the fiery trials that come your way. God has already warned us that they will come, but after you have suffered a little while (during the first onset of Satan's attacks), God does promise victory if we follow hisinstructions that he sets forth in his Word and faint not.

1 Peter 4:12 states, "Beloved [web: dearly loved] do not be amazed and bewildered [web: cause to lose one's bearings or be confused] at the fiery [web: being in an inflamed state or condition] ordeal which is taking place to test your quality as though something strange [unusual and alien to you and your position] were befalling you."

God specifically addresses these trials here and does not want us to be surprised, confused or shaken when they come. He also states that it is to test our quality or our character. Note: You will *NEVER* grow with God unless you are tested.

Remember what I stated previously about Satan accusing the brethren day and night?

Revelation 12:10 states, "Then I heard a strong [loud] voice in heaven saying, Now it is come-the salvation and the power and the Kingdom [the dominion, the reign] of our God and the power [the sovereignty, the authority] of his Christ [the Messiah] for the accuser of our brethren, [Satan] who keeps bringing before our God charges against them day and night has been cast out!"

You see, Satan actually is in contact with God and tells God things like: Let me attack them with this or with that (something he schemes up in secret) and then let's see if they will still follow, trust, or worship you? These are times of testing. We want to make sure we pass those tests by being obedient to what God says! Note: There is coming a day when Satan will be cast out forever, and we will no longer have his influences in our minds or hearts; but until then, we must use our spiritual warfare against him! (God's Word)

JOB'S TIME OF TESTING

The recording of the book of Job was given to us as an example of these times of testing that God speaks of. Let's read the account in the book of Job.

Job 1:8-11 states, "And the Lord said to Satan, Have you considered my servant Job, that there is none like him on the earth, a blameless and upright man, one who [reverently] fears God and abstains from and shuns evil [because it is wrong]." (v. 8)

"Then Satan answered the Lord, Does Job [reverently] fear God for nothing?" (v. 9)

"Have you not put a hedge about him and his house and all that he has, on every side? You have conferred prosperity and happiness upon him in the work of his hands and his possessions have increased in the land." (v. 10)

Here, Satan tells God, "Of course, Job fears you, but it hasn't been for nothing. It's because of all the blessings you have given him and your hedge of protection around him." Then, Satan continues in verse 11, telling God that if he takes away all Job has, he will certainly curse God.

"But put forth your hand now and touch all that he has and he will curse you to your face." (v. 11)

Job was indeed now under trial, and his character or quality was now being tested as it speaks of in 1 Peter 4:12. Well, Job did have everything taken away and was left with nothing. Yet, even after losing all he had possessed, Job still did not curse God. What did Job do in this trial and times of testing?

Job 1:20–22 states, "Then Job arose and rent [or tore] his robe and shaved his head and fell down upon the ground and worshipped." (v. 20)

Job still continued to worship God even in the midst of his trial! This is what God expects us to do. Remember, this is for our learning.

"And said, Naked [without possessions] came I [into this world] from my mother's womb and naked [without possessions] shall I depart. The Lord gave and the Lord has taken away; blessed [praised and magnified in worship] be the name of the Lord." (v. 21)

"In all this Job sinned not nor charged God foolishly." (v. 22)

Even though Job had been going through a fiery trial, yet amid all these things, he still remained faithful and kept his focus on God in praise. Then, Satan appears to God a second time.

Job 2:3–7 states, "And the Lord said to Satan, Have you considered My servant Job, that there is none like him on the earth, a blameless and upright man, one who [reverently] fears God and abstains from and shuns all evil [because it is wrong]? And he still holds fast his integrity [web: an unimpaired condition, firm adherence to a code of moral values] although you moved me against him to destroy him without cause." (v. 3)

God tells Satan that even through Job's trials, when everything was taken away, Job still remained in the same state as he was before by holding true to his integrity even though Job did nothing to deserve what had happened.

We need to take note and pay close attention here as God gives us the story of Job for us to follow as an example of what to do when trials come and when our character is being tested.

"Then, Satan answered the Lord, Skin for Skin! Yes, all that a man has will he give for his life." (v. 4)

"But put forth your hand now and touch his bone and his flesh and he will curse and renounce [web: refuse to follow, obey, or recognize any further] you to your face." (v. 5)

Now, Satan tells God, "Okay, let me attack his body and his flesh, thinking he will lose his life, and he will surely refuse to follow or obey you then."

Do you see how Satan relentlessly accuses Job? He does the same to us and that is why we need to just stay faithful and obedient to God during trials. There are many things going on behind the scenes, things we cannot see but need to trust that God knows what he is doing and just pass our times of testing.

The Lord then gives Satan permission to touch Job's health.

"And the Lord said to Satan, Behold, he is in your hand; only spare his life." (v. 6)

Talk about times of testing under trial! But God promises blessings as we stay faithful!

"So Satan went forth from the presence of the Lord an smote [web: attacked or afflicted suddenly] Job with loathsome and painful sores, from sole of his foot to the crown of his head." (v. 7)

Have you ever felt an attack come upon you suddenly as Job did? Well, this is nothing new, and we need not fear when it comes. Just recognize the source of where the attack is coming from (Satan, our enemy), then trust God to see you through it!

Of course, Job, being human as we all are, becomes very discouraged even to the point where he cursed the day he was born as seen in chapter 3.

Job 3:1 states, "After this, Job opened his mouth and cursed his day [birthday]."

In all this, Job still never once sinned or cursed God or refused to obey him during his trial. Even Job's friends turned against him and blamed Job during these great calamities, which angered God. Job still remained faithful to God even in all his opposition of great, intense pain and suffering. So faithful, that he even prayed for his friends who were accusing him. After Job had prayed for his friends, God over-turned the captivity and blessed him.

Job 42:4 states, "And the Lord turned the captivity of Job and restored his fortunes when he prayed for his friends; also the Lord gave Job twice as much as he had before."

This is a huge lesson we must learn here as believers. What will you do when fiery trials come upon you? When the testing of your character comes? Are you going to falter as Satan desires, leading to your own destruction or are you going to stand in obedience to and for God, not wavering in times of opposition which will lead to victory?

When trials come in your life, say over and over aloud: I'm going to pass this test! And look at it as a test with victory on the horizon.

Let's go back to the book of Peter.

1 Peter 4:13 states, "But insofar as you are sharing Christ's sufferings, rejoice [web: to feel joy or great delight] so when his glory [full of radiance and splendor] is revealed, you may also rejoice with triumph [exultantly]."

THIS IS THE WORD OF THE LORD

Hebrews 4:12–16 states, "For the Word that God speaks is alive and full of power [making it active; operative, energizing, and effective]. It is sharper than any two edged sword, penetrating to the dividing line of the breath of life [soul] and [the immortal] spirit and of joints and marrow [of the deepest parts of our nature] exposing and sifting and analyzing and judging the very thoughts and purposes of the heart." (v. 12)

Note: God says his Word is *ALIVE* and full of *POWER*—power to overcome *ANY* obstacle that comes our way!

"And not a creature exists that is concealed from his sight, but all things are open and exposed, naked and defenseless to the eyes of Him with whom we have to do." (v. 13)

God sees all he has created, and nothing is hidden from him. He knows how weak we all are and knows that without him, we are powerless over the opposing forces of darkness.

"Inasmuch then as we have a great High Priest who has [already] ascended and passed through the heavens, Jesus the son of God, let us hold fast our confession [of faith in him]." (v. 14)

"For we do not have a High Priest who is unable to understand and sympathize and have a shared feeling with our weaknesses and infirmities [web: state of being weak of mind, will or character] and liability to the assaults of temptation, but one who has been tempted in every aspect as we are, yet without sinning." (v. 15)

"Let us then fearlessly and confidently and boldly draw near to the throne of grace [the throne of God's unmerited or undeserved favor to us sinners], that we may receive mercy [for our failures] and find grace to help in good time for every need [appropriate help and well-timed help, coming just when we need it]." (v. 16)

Amen.

My hopes and prayers for everyone reading this book are that it will open up your spiritual eyes to see the truth that God has set forth in his Word which is addressed to us all, his children. That as you follow his instructions of how to do spiritual warfare, God would open up those prison doors that have kept you bound, and you too will achieve great victories and freedom in your life, a freedom from fear and panic stopping you from being all you can be. You too can begin to tap into a life that's flowing in abundance that your Heavenly Father so desires for you to have, a life that Jesus, our Lord and Savior, died for. In the name of Jesus, amen.

JESUS INSTRUCTED US TO PRAY AS FOLLOWS:

Matthew 6:5–13 states, "Also when you pray, you must not be like the hypocrites, for they love to pray standing in the synagogues and on the corners of the streets, that they may be seen by people. Truly, I tell you, they have their reward already." (v. 5)

"But when you pray, go into your [most] private room and closing the door, pray to your Father, Who is in secret; and your Father, Who sees in secret, will reward you in the open." (v. 6)

"And when you pray do not heap up phrases [multiply words, repeating the same ones over and over] as the Gentiles do, for they think they will be heard for their much speaking." (v. 7)

"Do not be like them, for your Father knows what you need before you ask him." (v. 8)

"Pray therefore, like this: Our Father Who is in Heaven, Hallowed [kept holy] be Your name." (v. 9)

"Your Kingdom come, Your will be done on earth as it is in heaven." (v. 10)

"Give us this day our daily bread." (v. 11) This is about talking about meeting our needs for that particular day.

"And forgive us our debts [web: sins or trespasses], as we also have forgiven [left, remitted, and let go of the debts and have given up resentment against them] our debtors [web: one guilty of neglect or violation of duty]." (v. 12)

"And lead [bring] us not into temptation, but deliver us from the evil one." (v. 13)

In the name of Jesus, Amen.

WEBSTER DICTIONARY

During my studies and research, I felt led by our Lord to use the *Webster Dictionary* as a tool to help clarify some definitions in scripture. I might add that I was very shocked and amazed at how what I originally thought the meanings of some words were totally different after my research.

The man who wrote the first *Webster Dictionary* was named Noah Webster, born in 1758 in West Hartford, Connecticut, and attended Yale University–Yale College. Noah's first publication of the dictionary was published in 1806, containing 37,000 words and went on to publish two more the following year. He spent the rest of his life, cataloging words and in 1828, he completed his final dictionary with seventy thousand words.

Noah was a Christian and was raised by his deacon father and began to learn the Bible at a very young age. He was known as the Father of American Education, a revolutionary soldier, a judge, legislator, and American founder.

On December 20, 1808, Noah had written a letter to Thomas Dawes who held prominent positions in the Massachusetts's government.

"About a year ago, an unusual revival of religion took place in New Haven.... and I was lead by a spontaneous impulse of repentance, prayer, and entire submission of myself to my Maker and Redeemer. In the mouth of April last, I made a profession of faith. This unusual revival was part of the Great Awakening that shook America in the early nineteenth century."

Noah went on and completed a textbook, *History of the United States*, published in 1832. His belief was that of Christianity and government could not and should not be ever separated as he quoted in his book,

"The religion which has introduced civil liberty is the religion of Christ and His apostles, which enjoins humility, piety, and benevolence; which acknowledges in every person, a brother or sister, and a citizen with equal rights. This is genuine Christianity, and to this we owe our free constitutions of government."

Then, he also quoted,

"Every Civil government is based upon some religion or philosophy of life. Education in a nation will propagate the religion of that nation. In America, the foundational religion was Christianity, and it was sown in the hearts of Americans through the home and private and public schools for centuries. Our liberty, growth and prosperity was the result of a biblical philosophy of life. Our continued freedom and success is dependent on our educating the youth of America in the principles of Christianity."

I believe during Noah's research and writings, God had intervened in his life, giving him a spiritual awakening. I believe God worked hand in hand with Noah to give real and true spiritual meanings to the words written in *The Webster Dictionary*.

God had shown Noah that his Word (the Bible) is truth for which Noah also quoted, "The Bible must be considered as the great source of all the truth by which men are to be guided in government as well as in all social transactions."

ABOUT THE AUTHOR

Grace Nichols was born in 1958 in Milford, Connecticut. She was called to serve as a missionary in Southern California and is recently relocated to San Tan Valley, Arizona. She is a single mother of two grown daughters. Her life's goal and desire has always been to help others through and with God, as the Lord leads. Her beliefs are to seek out answers through the Word of God and that he has given us his Word (the Bible) to address any and all life's troubles.

"Just as a Father instructs his children of whom he loves, how could our Heavenly Father not do the same for us?" Her firm belief is God gave us his Word (the Bible), as God's instruction book to us all. She has sought God out through his Word to give aid not only to herself, but also to help others unfold the many secrets and mysteries. God opens the eyes of those of us who give initiative to delve deep into the things written therein. Exposing those things and leaving no doubt to the human mind will lead us all to freedom and a life flowing in abundance.

CPSIA information can be obtained
at www.ICGtesting.com
Printed in the USA
FSOW01n1741200217
30943FS

9 781681 979007